Stitch BY Stitch

Stitch BY Stitch

LEARNING TO SEW, ONE PROJECT AT A TIME

by deborah moebes

kp

KRAUSE PUBLICATIONS
CINCINNATI, OHIO

Stitch by Stitch. Copyright © 2010 by Deborah Moebes. Manufactured in China. All rights reserved. The patterns and drawings in this book are for the personal use of the reader. By permission of the author and publisher, they may be either hand-traced or photocopied to make single copies, but under no circumstances may they be resold or republished. No other part of this book may be reproduced in any form or by any electronic or mechanical means including information storage and retrieval systems without permission in writing from the publisher, except by a reviewer who may quote brief passages in a review. Published by Krause Publications, an imprint of F+W Media, Inc., 4700 East Galbraith Road, Cincinnati, Ohio, 45236. (800) 289-0963. First Edition.

17 16 15 14 13   8 7 6 5 4

Distributed in Canada by Fraser Direct
100 Armstrong Avenue
Georgetown, ON, Canada L7G 5S4
Tel: (905) 877-4411

Distributed in the U.K. and Europe by David & Charles
Brunel House, Newton Abbot, Devon, TQ12 4PU, England
Tel: (+44) 1626 323200, Fax: (+44) 1626 323319
Email: postmaster@davidandcharles.co.uk

Distributed in Australia by Capricorn Link
P.O. Box 704, S. Windsor NSW, 2756 Australia
Tel: (02) 4577-3555

Library of Congress Cataloging in Publication Data
Moebes, Deborah.
  Stitch by stitch : learning to sew, one project at a time / by Deborah Moebes. -- 1st ed.
      p. cm.
  Includes bibliographical references and index.
  ISBN 978-1-4402-1161-4 (hardback : alk. paper)
  1. Machine sewing. I. Title.
TT705.M593 2010
646.2'044--dc22
                              2010006894

METRIC CONVERSION CHART		
To convert	to	multiply by
Inches	Centimeters	2.54
Centimeters	Inches	0.4
Feet	Centimeters	30.5
Centimeters	Feet	0.03
Yards	Meters	0.9
Meters	Yards	1.1

www.fwmedia.com

CREDITS
Thanks to *Sweetwater* for use of their fabric design on the pages in this book.

EDITED BY
KRISTIN BOYS

DESIGNED BY
KELLY O'DELL

PRODUCTION COORDINATED BY
GREG NOCK

STEP-BY-STEP PHOTOGRAPHY BY
CHRISTINE POLOMSKY

COVER PHOTOGRAPHY BY
AL PARRISH

ALL OTHER PHOTOGRAPHY BY
RIC DELIANTONI

DEDICATION

For Sandra, who unknowingly put my feet on this path, and for Michael, who lovingly kept them there.

ACKNOWLEDGMENTS

This book was a ton of work, and there is simply no way it would ever have come into existence without a similar amount of love and support from a whole pile of people. A special thanks goes to: All the students who have come through my sewing classes over the past three years and who have asked the questions and stitched the projects that helped me refine the content of this book—I wouldn't have even embarked on this project had you not made it clear that there was a need! Elle and Courtney, who forced me to drag my dreams out of the dark and convinced me they were totally worth it. Readers of my blog, who have commented and supported me as I worked to find a voice in my writing. Beehive Co-op, which has been my home and launching pad during this whole process. My editors, Kristin and Vanessa, who have been tireless and kind and super supportive throughout. Finally, heartfelt thanks to all my family, who never doubted me for a second.

CONTENTS

LETTER TO THE STITCHER

Dear you,

I want you to really love sewing. I guess that's the most honest way to start. I hope you jump in and find that learning to sew is wonderful and enjoyable and rewarding and empowering and inspiring and fun. I totally feel that way and can't imagine my life without the certain knowledge that I can "make stuff."

I've been teaching sewing classes for years now, and I'm heartbroken each time someone comes through the doors and tells me that they've taken a class before but felt so belittled or intimidated or condescended to that they were turned off from sewing forever. If nothing else, I want this book to be the opposite of that. I truly believe anyone can sew (and I secretly think everyone should). It's super important to me that this be your happy place, and that you discover inspiration and possibility in sewing that you always hoped you'd find.

I've written this not only for beginning sewers, but for what I call "returning sewers," too. You are the folks who've taught yourselves a little, or who took classes years and years ago, or who've been making it up for so long that you really feel there's an easier way to do things. I will start at the very beginning here, but the content of this book moves quickly into varsity territory, because I figure there are plenty of people like me: impatient to get to the good stuff. I want you to be motivated and excited to keep going, and I want you to have results that you can show off right away.

I'm truly excited that you're here. Thank goodness! I can't wait to get to know you better and see what you'll create.

With excited anticipation,

Deborah

9

SOME NOTES ON USING THIS BOOK

As you work through each project, you'll notice I tend to refer back to projects that have come before. That's because the book really is intended to be used that way: as a whole. I adore so many of the sewing books out there and am deeply inspired and excited by the gorgeous, hip, clever projects they present. Many of them, though, gloss over the essentials of sewing or simply assume too much knowledge to allow you to be successful as you work through their ideas. When they do include basic sewing instruction, it's often divorced from the projects themselves, making it hard for you to determine where and when you'd use the various tools and techniques. I want this book to be different for you—you know, better.

I'm well aware that many folks who come to sewing have come with some degree of previous knowledge. That's great! I also know that others come with absolutely nothing but a fervent desire to create with fabric and machine. That's awesome! This book is for all of you. I've included all the basics I've developed during my years of teaching individuals of all ability levels to sew, and I've integrated some really cool, more advanced ideas and techniques as we go. That way, even if you feel as though some of the information is review, there is always something new and fun to learn as you work your way through the projects. If you really want to skip around, golly, there are no cops to stop you! I do hope you'll at least skim all the pages, though; I'm pretty sure you'll find a lot there you'll like.

"Many folks who come to sewing have come with some degree of previous knowledge. That's great! I also know that others come with absolutely nothing but a fervent desire to create with fabric and machine. That's awesome! This book is for all of you."

HOW I CAME TO LOVE SEWING–A LOT

I didn't always sew. Well, in a way I suppose I did: My mother sews, and her mother before her, and her mother before her, and on and on, so I had a needle and thread in hand from a very early age. But I was pretty resistant to learning from my mom. She taught me the mechanics of the machine and the needle, but I think I always felt I knew more than she did (or at least, more than she gave me credit for), so I don't think I heard everything she had to teach. If my sewing students are to be believed, this is not an uncommon dynamic between mothers and daughters.

Then I went to college. Working in the university costume shop at the School of Theatre, I was exposed to a whole new world of sewing: new rules, new techniques, new fabrics, new philosophy. I had always thought of sewing as utilitarian, but here I was introduced to folks who were sewing on sequins by hand and custom-fitting garments that would be put into storage for years after a scant twenty minutes on stage. I wondered why on earth they would take the trouble, and it dawned on me that they did so out of love for the act of creation itself and out of excitement for the work and the final product. I had thought I understood what sewing was about, but it turns out I'd only seen one side and had missed out on the sheer delight that creating can bring. I found out I knew some sewing techniques, but not all, and I discovered a real love for the craft.

I taught high school, including costume design, for eight years after completing my degree and have taught adults to sew since 2006. I guess my point in sharing my pedigree is to say this isn't my first square dance. I've spent years looking for great ideas and projects and places and techniques to teach people not just to sew, but to really enjoy sewing. In that time, though, what I didn't discover was a good sewing teacher. I became frustrated over and over again with books and classes that claimed to be for beginners but that left out the most important details.

I *looooove* sewing, and I feel actual pain when I hear people say how they wanted to learn but were turned off by a mean teacher or a frustrating tutorial. I want to offer new stitchers that same love and excitement without the pain and drama. That's what this book does: It provides a new approach to learning to sew that allows you to achieve (nearly) instant gratification by creating cute projects right away, but also sneaks essential instruction into each of those projects so you're learning foundational skills as you go. I hope that as you learn new techniques and ideas—and make projects you'll be proud to show off—you'll discover the joy of creating and the excitement that comes from a project well done.

SEWING: THEN AND NOW

Why We Sew

Throughout human history, sewing has been an essential necessity. Constructing clothing and shelter from animal hides, weaving and spinning fibers into cloth to be stitched, creating containers and bags for carrying and storing essentials have all been accomplished with needle, awl, thread and skill. Our modern world affords us the luxury of avoiding the need to sew as a means simply to clothe ourselves and allows us remarkable access to ready-to-wear clothing, crafts and home decor. In recent years, though, we've seen a huge increase in the number of individuals worldwide who are motivated to sew, create, craft and mold fabric into new forms. Why the surge, and what does it reflect about us?

Sewing Today: Rebirth

The Craft Gap. That's what I call my theory of why crafting—and sewing specifically—seems to suddenly be everywhere all the time: blogs, the news, street fairs, online shops, all over.

Sewing has always been around. In my former life as an archaeologist, I spent plenty of time looking at the physical evidence—material culture, we called it—of how women lived in the past. These lives have always included sewing implements: needles, awls, hooks, pins. So the perception that sewing is new is false. But it feels so new, so *now*—why is that? And what has caused sewing and crafting to suddenly become the hip thing to do?

My hypothesis is that we're witness to the crest of a generation who didn't have crafting and sewing as a central part of their experience. I call it the Craft Gap. Born anywhere from about 1965 to 1990 or so, we

HISTORY OF MACHINE SEWING: A TIMELINE

1790
Thomas Saint issues a British patent for a sewing machine. It doesn't work.

1810
German Balthasar Krems invents a machine to sew caps. He doesn't patent it. It doesn't work so great, either.

1814
Austrian tailor Josef Madersperger receives a patent for a sewing machine. It never works well.

1818
The first American patent issued for a sewing machine. It sews a few stitches and then malfunctions.

1834
Hunt invents America's first more-or-less successful sewing machine. He doesn't bother to patent it. He fears it will drive seamstresses out of work.

1836
Elias Howe receives the first American patent for a machine that "uses thread from two sources." Finally!

1850s
Isaac Singer invents a machine with an up-and-down motion rather than side-to-side. It's a huge hit and a big improvement.

didn't have sewing presented to us as a viable, valuable outlet for creativity. Now, I'm not saying that no one born in those years ever learned to sew. Obviously that's not the case, or I wouldn't be sewing today. I am saying, though, that there was a distinctly different attitude toward sewing after the mid-1960s than there had been in the past. 4-H programs were fewer in number, home ec classes were disappearing all over, and fewer moms and grandmothers were passing on their skills, either because they were less involved in sewing themselves or because we were less interested in picking up a craft that was increasingly viewed as dowdy and out of touch.

This has left us with a whole generation—mostly of women, but certainly of men, too—who don't have the background and the years of experience that our predecessors did. And there seems to be some part of us that misses it.

These days, as I teach sewing classes, I hear student after student repeat these same ideas to me: I always wanted to learn but never knew where to go; my mom/grandmother/aunt wanted to teach me but I wasn't interested; I took home ec but haven't done it in so long that I feel like I don't remember anything. And all of us, me included, have this sense that there is a richness lacking from our day-to-day lives as a result, that having this creative outlet, challenge, inspiration and accomplishment would make us feel more satisfied, connected and a part of something lasting. Sewing allows us to do that, and learning these skills gives us a connection to the past, to our own creativity, to our children and to others who share our vision.

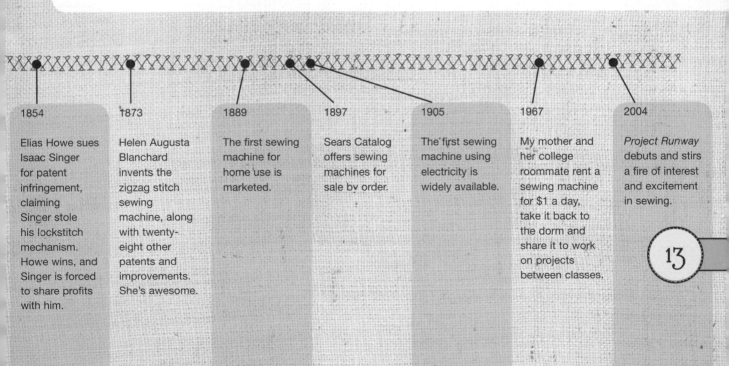

1854

Elias Howe sues Isaac Singer for patent infringement, claiming Singer stole his lockstitch mechanism. Howe wins, and Singer is forced to share profits with him.

1873

Helen Augusta Blanchard invents the zigzag stitch sewing machine, along with twenty-eight other patents and improvements. She's awesome.

1889

The first sewing machine for home use is marketed.

1897

Sears Catalog offers sewing machines for sale by order.

1905

The first sewing machine using electricity is widely available.

1967

My mother and her college roommate rent a sewing machine for $1 a day, take it back to the dorm and share it to work on projects between classes.

2004

Project Runway debuts and stirs a fire of interest and excitement in sewing.

13

THE MODERN SEAMSTRESS

Who Is Today's Sewer?

In so many people's heads, sewing is still the realm of the The Little Olde Lady. If you've taken the briefest peek at the Internet lately, though, you've quickly learned how untrue that stereotype has become. Television shows like *Project Runway,* independent films like *Handmade Nation* and the many, many cool craft blogs out there reveal a whole world of sewing and crafting that didn't exist ten years ago.

As a result, the demographics of "today's sewer" have changed dramatically. In my classes, I see primarily women between the ages of twenty-five and forty-five, but we get a lot of teens and tweens, as well as a few older women who were so liberated they simply never learned to sew. We get plenty of men, too, with goals as lofty as any of the ladies.

Most of these folks are intelligent, educated and curious, and have fantastic ideas of their own. Many of them have searched and searched for home decor and clothing that satisfies their taste without breaking the bank, or that suits their unique worldview, and have been unsuccessful; for them, sewing represents an opportunity to bring their vision to life.

Folks who sew today want to work on something creative, connect with others who share their vision and have a tangible product when they're done. They're not usually in the market for the duckies-and-bunnies-on-rollerskates aesthetic our grandmothers are so fond of (mine is notorious for her immaculately crafted cross-stitched sweatshirts bearing images of the duck decoys my grandfather carves). Instead, today's sewing is edgy and funky; it combines new and vintage materials to amazing effect; and it reflects the ideals and desires of a whole new culture, a crafting culture.

Yes, today's sewer is one hip individual.

What's a "Sewist"?

Much has been made of the differences between the "sewer" and "sewist." I love that both these words are out there, and I love what they represent. For some, a "sewer" is one who sews, but there is not necessarily the implication of exceptional skill, just that the person enjoys needle and thread, and perhaps is still in the process of learning. By that definition, a "sewist" is a true craftsperson, an artist with fabric and thread, who creates something new and original and gorgeous. I think many of those who stitch are aspiring sewists, but I want to caution you if you see any shame in being a sewer: Everyone starts at the beginning, as you are now. Be bold! Excellence comes with experience, young grasshopper.

The sewist, the artist who sews, has always been around. Sewing is and has always been part art, part craft: something we can use that is also something of beauty that reflects our values, pride, desires and hopes. You are part of that, as well! By picking up needle and thread, you are part of something bigger and are connected to both the past and the future; you are part of a long line stretching on and on, and are tied to others you haven't even met yet. You may think all you're doing is making some stitches, but really, you're doing so much more! Embrace the new you, the sewing you, and be proud to be beginning a journey you might never have expected. I know I certainly didn't think when I was sewing to relieve the stress of working on a graduate degree that it would become my whole life. It has, and I am so, so grateful. I want you to feel the same level of joy and excitement when you sew, and I sincerely hope this book is a place where you can start.

> "Sewing is and has always been part art, part craft: something we can use that is also something of beauty that reflects our values, pride, desires and hopes. You are part of that, as well! By picking up needle and thread, you are part of something bigger and are connected to both the past and the future."

Time for Reflection

Now, I know you're probably thinking, "Enough of the anthropological lessons, let's get sewing!" I get it. But I truly think that assessing where you're at and where you want to go will help you establish a good foundation for starting (or continuing) to sew. You don't want to dive willy nilly into the sewing pool and find yourself starting to drown.

Sewing History

History has a tendency to repeat itself. So, think about your own history with the machine to help you start fresh and avoid repeating bad behaviors and disasters.

Where'd you come from, and what took you so long to get here?

_____

_____

_____

What's been keeping you from sewing? Was it a bad experience?

_____

_____

_____

**What's your worst sewing nightmare? What fear(s) has prevented you
from adding skills before now?**

_____

_____

_____

Inspiration

Like any other craft, sewing is creative, and creativity requires inspiration to stay motivated. Consider these questions to determine what will keep you inspired.

Who most inspires you to get creating with needle and thread? Is a mother or grandmother, or having your first child or sending your kids off and having more time to sew for yourself?

_____

_____

_____

What gets you itching to use that machine?

_____

_____

_____

Goals

I don't intend to take you back to your last painful dating or job interview experience ("Where do you see yourself in 10 years?"). But thinking about where you want to go will make it easier for you to start. Goal-setting will keep you from becoming overwhelmed with everything you want do, and help you see what you are really accomplishing (which will be more than you realize!).

What are your sewing goals? What skills would you like to learn? What would you like to see yourself sewing regularly, after you have the skills? At what level do you expect to see yourself in a month? Three months? A year?

_____

_____

_____

_____

List the three things you'd like to be able to create by the time you've completed the lessons in this book. They can be projects (like a pillow for the sofa or a skirt for yourself), skills (like learning to make pleats or add piping) or experiences (make something I'm proud to give as a gift or have three garments for myself hanging in the closet).

_____

_____

_____

_____

_____

_____

Let's say time, skill and money are no object. What is the one project you most want to create?

_____

_____

_____

_____

Now that you've thought a little about yourself, you might want to share it with others. Talk to your mom or best friend about what you learned. Hey—maybe they'll even give you valuable feedback. Read and comment on sewing blogs and get involved in the sewing community (see Resources and Inspiration on pages 216–217). It will help keep you motivated and reflecting on your sewing life.

PART ONE:
GETTING STARTED

GET THE GOODS:
TOOLS & MATERIALS

To join in with this crafty movement, and to be part of that bigger wave that sewing embodies, you need to start at the beginning: the tools of sewing. For every technique or sewing method out there, I've found multiple products that promise to do the task. Because I tend to be both frugal and forgetful, though, I'm the least likely person to hop out of my chair and run to the store for some product I forgot to buy the last time I was there. The supplies I highlight in the next pages are the ones I think of immediately any time I am asked what I consider to be essential sewing equipment. In fact, this is almost precisely the list I developed on the fly when I taught my first sewing class, and in the intervening years I've found few products so great that they have been added to the list. Isn't it great to learn that sometimes simple really does do the trick?

ONE

TWO TOOLS TO INVEST IN

Sewing, when you get right down to it, is just taking the ugly, cut edges of fabric and making them pretty. That means that cutting and pressing are super important—in fact, I often say that sewing is 90 percent cutting and 60 percent pressing, which makes it about negative 50 percent stitching. That should be good news! It means that even if stitching is your weakest skill, you can still get really excellent results as long as you cut well and press often.

In order to do that, you'll need good equipment. I recommend investing money in two places before investing it anywhere else, and neither of them is in the machine. First is an excellent pair of scissors, and second is your iron.

Scissors

For sewing, you'll be using a pair of scissors called shears. Regular scissors have two round holes, while shears have one round hole for the thumb and an oblong hole for fingers, which allows greater stability when cutting fabric. Most folks start out using the basic orange plastic-handled shears. There is absolutely nothing wrong with those scissors. They have one major drawback, though: Because they're made with aluminum blades, they can't be sharpened when they dull (which all scissors do, eventually). What this means, ultimately, is that they're disposable scissors, which you'll need to replace when they start chewing your fabric with their dull edges. Although it may seem more economical to purchase them at the outset, compared to another pair that may cost four times as much, replacing them over and over will negate those savings pretty quickly.

Now, if you have a pair of these scissors, you don't have to throw them out and then run out and get a fancy pair! Keep using them until they no longer meet your needs long; anything much bigger can be unwieldy.

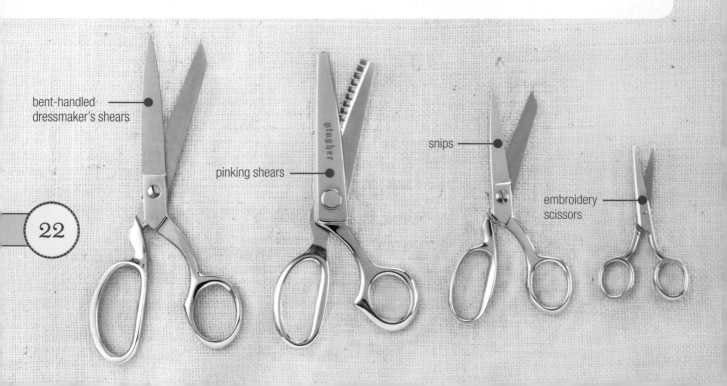

bent-handled dressmaker's shears

pinking shears

snips

embroidery scissors

These puppies are true scissors: There are two of them, connected by a nut-and-bolt assembly (each handle-and-blade is a single piece, and each is a "scissor"). That means the steel can be sharpened, and the solid, one-piece construction will make these last well beyond your lifetime. Although it might seem you want a lighter pair of scissors, in actuality, the weight of a heavy, steel pair will assist you in cutting because gravity will be doing a large part of the work (as opposed to those lighter-weight scissors, which force you to bear down in order to get anything done).

Iron

When I graduated from college and got my first "real job," I went out and bought myself an iron, y'know, to iron my work clothes. Never mind that I already had two degrees and a child of my own; buying that iron made me feel I'd entered into adulthood. The iron I purchased, though, was evaluated on different criteria than what you ought to use when buying an iron for sewing. It had an aluminum sole plate with a nonstick coating and was very lightweight. Since then, I've learned that a thin aluminum plate is lightweight to reduce fatigue, but the irony is that to really compress the fabric, I need more weight, not less. See, ironing and pressing aren't the same thing, and in sewing, we want to press more than iron, making a heavier iron more effective.

My new iron has a stainless steel sole plate, no nonstick coating—which I don't really need because I use very little starch—and is heavier. I have to use a lot less elbow grease to get the same results. Like any other serious piece of equipment (lawn mowers, hedge trimmers), it's wise to buy the best iron you can afford, rather than an inexpensive one that will just get hot. You'll feel the difference and get better results. On top of that, it will last longer and work harder for you. Should you throw out your current iron? That's not neccessary. But when the iron you have has gone on one too many dates with the floor from the cat knocking it off the ironing board, invest in a solid iron you'll use for years and years.

Shopping List + Supplies: Basic Sewing Tools

For each project in the book, I provide you with a list of supplies, along with all the tools you'll need to complete the project. Nearly every sewing project (in the book, and in life) requires a set of the same essential tools. So, in the Shopping List + Supplies lists for the projects, you'll see Basic Sewing Tools.

These include:
* sewing machine with standard presser foot
* sewing scissors
* iron and ironing board
* pins

THE ESSENTIALS: YOU WON'T GET MUCH DONE WITHOUT THESE

After you have the right scissors and iron, you can focus on getting a sweet sewing machine (see more on that in the next chapter). While you're browsing, though, you might want to look into these supplies, too.

Essential Tools

MARKING CHALK

You'll want something to mark fabric with, whether it's sketching out the dimensions of a pillow, transferring markings from a pattern piece or preparing to stitch buttonholes. Felt-tip markers are a bad bet, but outside of that, almost anything that'll transfer a mark without leaving a stain will do the job. There are piles of options: traditional tailor's chalk, disappearing ink pens, water-soluble ink pens, dressmaker's pencils or chalk cartridges. I like to use quilter's marking chalk (shown here) because it makes a clean, smooth line without wrinkling the fabric, and comes off easily with water. You'll find it in the quilting supplies section rather than the notions section.

SEAM RIPPER

So many people see the seam ripper as the scarlet letter of sewing, and view any need to use it with shame. Not so! How great is it that mistakes in sewing often can be fixed so simply, just by removing the stitches? Keep in mind that the sharpened blade of the seam ripper is only in the U-shaped part, not along the fingers. To remove stitches without tearing or distressing your fabric, slide the seam ripper point under every third stitch and cut with the blade, then pull the stitches from the fabric.

SEAM GUIDE

A seam guide is a small, metal gadget with a magnet beneath that allows it to stick to your throat plate. Because of its shape, it creates a "fence" against which to place the cut edge of your fabric as you sew, helping you get super straight stitching. Not everyone loves them, but many beginning sewers are really grateful for the extra help this guy can provide!

HEM GUIDE AND SEAM GAUGE

A hem guide is primarily intended to help you set the depth of a hem at the bottom of a skirt, dress or pants. There are a number of styles, and each is suited to different tasks. An aluminum hem guide allows the heat of your iron to radiate through it and reflect back to the garment, creating a super crisp press on both straight and curved hems. A seam gauge is small and lightweight, and also works well for setting hems as well as for adjusting patterns.

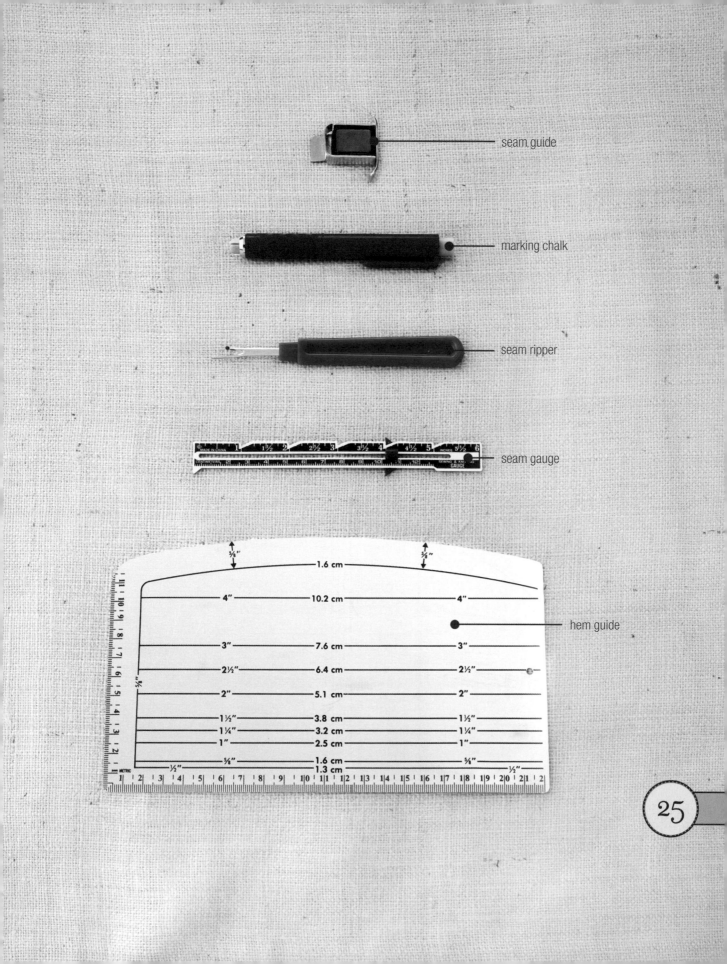

seam guide

marking chalk

seam ripper

seam gauge

hem guide

25

SPECIALTY PRESSER FEET

For almost any sewing task, there are specialty presser feet to make the job a little easier. For most stitching, you'll just need your standard presser foot, but a standard zipper foot and buttonhole foot are essential to stitching on zippers and crafting buttonholes, both of which you'll complete in chapter four.

EXTRA BOBBINS

You can never have too many bobbins. These little guys, used to hold additional thread below the needle and essential to the operation of your machine, seem to disappear every time you turn around. Having empty ones on hand prevents the horrifying waste of having to unwind and discard thread from a bobbin so you can rewind it with another color—oh, the horror! I always keep bobbins filled with black, white, natural, red and gray (gray is a fantastic neutral that will blend with most prints the others won't).

MEASURING TAPE

Standard measuring tapes are way better than a ruler: They're flexible (made of fiberglass or canvas), so they can wrap around your figure or be stretched along your fabric for accurate measurements. They're inexpensive enough that you can have two or three on hand at any time. I keep one in my purse to take with me to thrift and consignment stores, so I won't have to try things on.

PINCUSHION

There are so many different ways to store your pins that there is hardly space in this book to elaborate on all of them. I prefer the classic tomato—it has stood the test of time, and has handy sections for separating types of needles or pins. You might not realize that the strawberry pincushion works as a pin sharpener. My grandmother, Miriam, would say, "Oh, Debbie, what did you think it was for, decoration?" Yes, Grandma, I did think that. In fact, the strawberry is filled with emery powder (the same stuff on the emery boards you use to file your nails). The emery powder not only sharpens your pins when it abrades them, it also serves to remove any impurities the pins may have picked up, like oils from your skin or finishes from your fabric, which may damage your projects. (Emery pincushions were used historically to remove rusty bits from pins and needles, but here's hoping you won't need it for that purpose!)

If the tomato just isn't for you, there are plenty of other options: magnetic dishes that "catch" your pins as you work; sweet wooden boxes with magnetic tops to store and manage pins; wrist pincushions that allow you to have your pins right at hand; and even tiny dress forms with padding to allow you to stab your pins right into their little bodies. Who said sewing wasn't edgy?

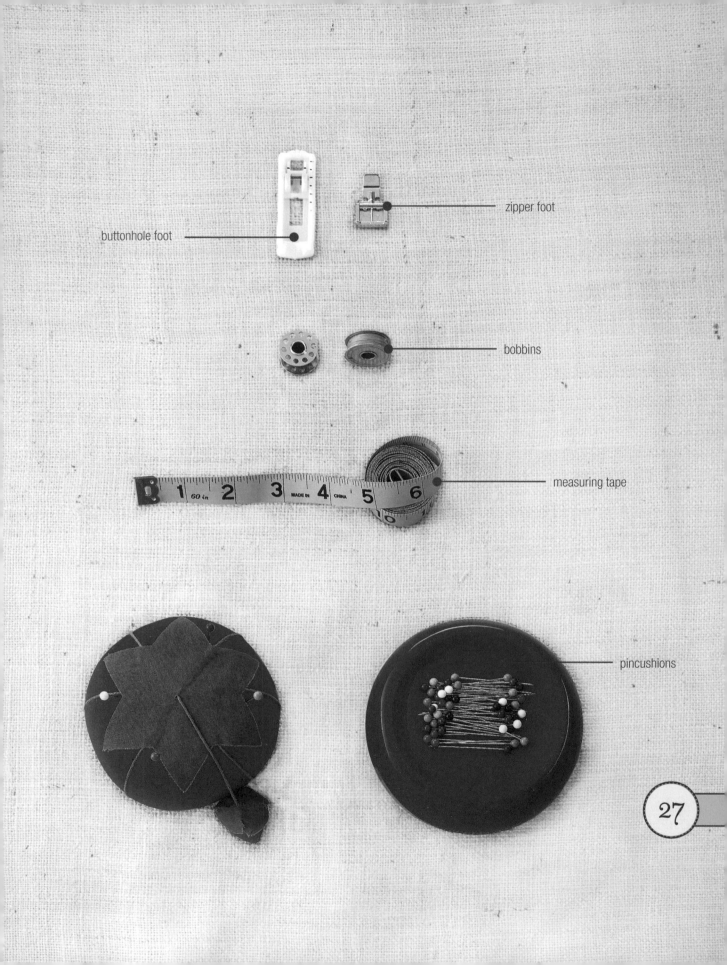

buttonhole foot

zipper foot

bobbins

measuring tape

pincushions

On Pins and Needles

Speaking of pins, here are all the types you might need.

STRAIGHT PINS

As you're working with fabric, you'll want to hold your pieces in place before stitching them together. Pins are perfect for this and come in so many varieties. Look for a good, universal pin: 1½ –2" (4cm–5cm) in length, made of steel (not nickel, since nickel can corrode and damage your fabrics). We'll talk later about sewing without pins, which some stitchers really, really love, but for those new to sewing, pins are tremendously helpful in building confidence.

Flat head pins are my mother's favorite. Her argument is that they have a slightly larger shaft and don't bend as easily as other pins, making them last longer. They're also the classic sewing pin, and are popular for that reason. After the time I stitched a flat head pin into my daughter's jumper side seam and sent her off to school, I switched to the ball head pin, which has a colored plastic or glass ball at the end opposite the point to make it more visible. Quilter's pins are very much like ball head pins, but slightly longer, allowing them to hold more layers of fabric at one time. Silk pins are slimmer and sharper than standard sewing pins, and their delicate diameter prevents them from leaving a lasting hole in fine fabrics after pinning. T-pins are fatter and sturdier, and are often used for upholstering and working with home decor fabrics.

SAFETY PINS

Straight pins have an exposed point that makes them quick and easy to work with for most sewing projects. Sometimes, though, you want to hold your work together for longer, or you need to avoid getting poked while you're stitching. Safety pins are great for this because of the enclosed hood. Use them to hold pieces of a quilt together, to thread elastic through a waistband casing, to adjust the side seams of a skirt as you fit it on yourself and for lots more tasks.

HAND SEWING NEEDLES

Most of us are familiar with needles for hand sewing: They have a pointed end, a smooth shank and an eye for carrying thread. They come in sizes and varieties based on the work they're intended for, and having a few different ones available is a good idea. You'll want them for finishing hems and facings, for embellishing your finished projects with appliqué or embroidery and for attaching buttons or hooks and eyes, among other things.

SEWING MACHINE NEEDLES

Unlike hand sewing needles, sewing machine needles have a shank that you insert into the machine and an eye in the tip of the needle, near the point. They do come in sizes, though, like hand sewing needles, and those sizes are related to the tasks to which they're suited. (Read more about machine needles on page 48.)

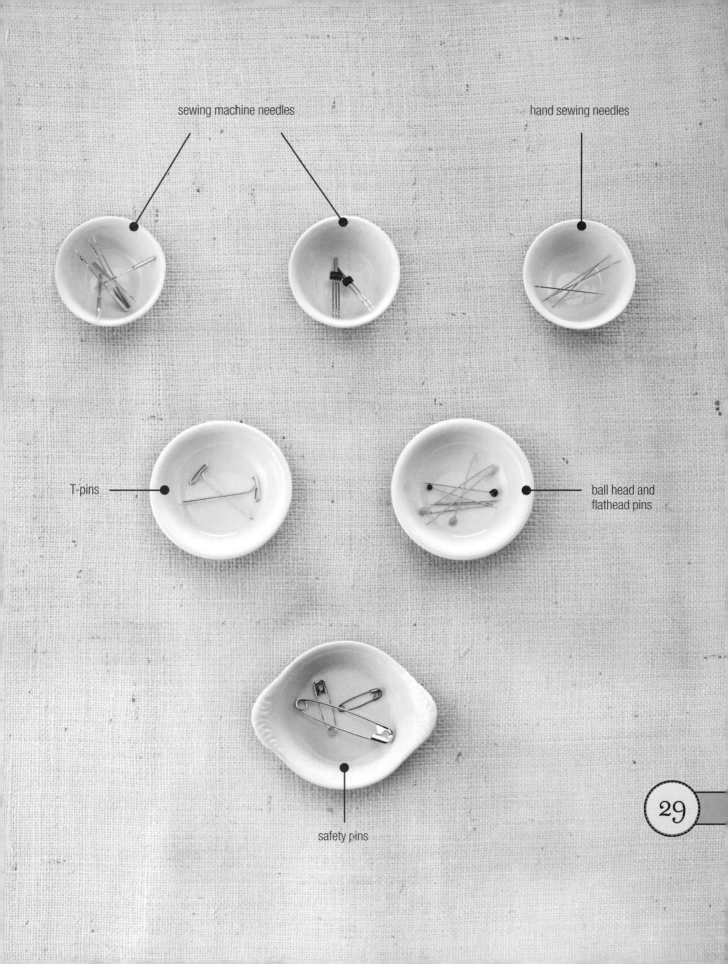

sewing machine needles

hand sewing needles

T-pins

ball head and flathead pins

safety pins

There's a Lot More to Thread Than You Thought

When shopping for thread, most folks just look for a good color match and call it a day. It's important to know that different threads are made for different purposes, and you'll get better results if you match your thread to the task you're asking it to perform.

COTTON-WRAPPED POLYESTER THREAD

This is your basic, all-purpose thread and is useful for most basic projects. The polyester inner core is protected from heat by the cotton overwrap, which gives the thread greater strength and durability.

100% POLYESTER THREAD

While slightly less durable than cotton thread, polyester threads will not stretch or shrink, making them another great all-purpose thread.

SILK THREAD

Silk threads are beautiful to look at and have a natural luster. Because of their amazing strength and durability, they are great for machine quilting and crafts.

UPHOLSTERY THREAD

This is a very heavyweight thread designed to handle a lot of stress and abuse. Much too heavy for most apparel applications, it's perfect for use with home decor and heavier fabrics.

EMBROIDERY THREAD

These are specialty threads designed for use in machine embroidery. Available in hundreds of colors and variations, this is usually a rayon thread that maintains its depth and shine after many washings. Be aware that embroidery floss for hand embroidery is grossly unsuited for machine sewing, but some machine embroidery threads can be used successfully for hand embroidery.

BASTING THREAD

When assembling a garment, stitchers often want to put the garment together and test the fit or make adjustments prior to putting in the final stitches. This process is called basting, and a special thread exists just for this purpose. It is thicker and coarser than all-purpose thread, making it easy to see. Plus, it breaks easily, allowing it to be snapped by hand so you can easily remove it after the final stitches are in place.

Choosing Thread Color

When you choose a thread color, remember that the color on the spool is always slightly darker than on the fabric. Unwind a bit of thread and lay it on your fabric: You want to match either the darkest color in the print, or the predominant color. You also want to choose the thread that best disappears into the fabric, in much the same way you would choose a foundation to match your skin tone.

YOU DON'T HAVE TO HAVE THESE, BUT THEY SURE DO HELP

CLEAR ACRYLIC RULER

There are any number of measuring devices out there, but my preference is the clear acrylic ruler. It allows you to see through to the fabric beneath and has markings at regular intervals, and some models include angles for cutting shapes. This ruler is also essential companion equipment to the rotary cutter because it provides a perfect straight edge against which to hold the rotary blade.

ROTARY CUTTER AND MAT

Rotary cutters are another quilting tool that is rapidly crossing over to the apparel sewing market. Basically a razor blade on a wheel, they're extraordinarily sharp, and because they don't require you to squeeze to create pressure when cutting, allow you to cut many more layers of fabric than scissors do. Large models can cut up to twenty layers of fabric at the same time, a huge benefit if you're cutting out umpteen million squares for a ginormous quilt or if you're making a zillion Christmas gifts and want to start a little assembly line at your work table.

The real drawback to rotary cutters is that they require a self-healing cutting mat beneath them, and those can be quite expensive. I resisted for ages, but can honestly say that I wouldn't want to work without my cutter now. Like good scissors, the blades on a rotary cutter can be sharpened, and if cared for, the mats can last for years.

SPECIALTY PRESSER FEET

The truth is, folks have been doing all of their sewing for decades with little more than a standard foot and a zipper foot, but there are some out now that are great to have around: An invisible zipper foot can increase the perfectness of your zipper installation; a dual-feed or walking foot can make working with slippery fabrics or plaids much easier; and a narrow hem foot is great if you plan to make a lot of ruffles or work with very fine fabrics.

KNITTING NEEDLE

Any project that needs to be turned right side out will need a little help, either by using a point to make all the seams nice and crisp or by turning the entire piece of fabric inside out. Lots of tools and toys are made to help with this, like loop turners and others, but I like to use my wooden knitting needle. It has a rounded point on one end that can be run in a seam to get a clean finish, and a ball end to glide smoothly along the inside of a tube of fabric to turn it quickly and neatly to the outside.

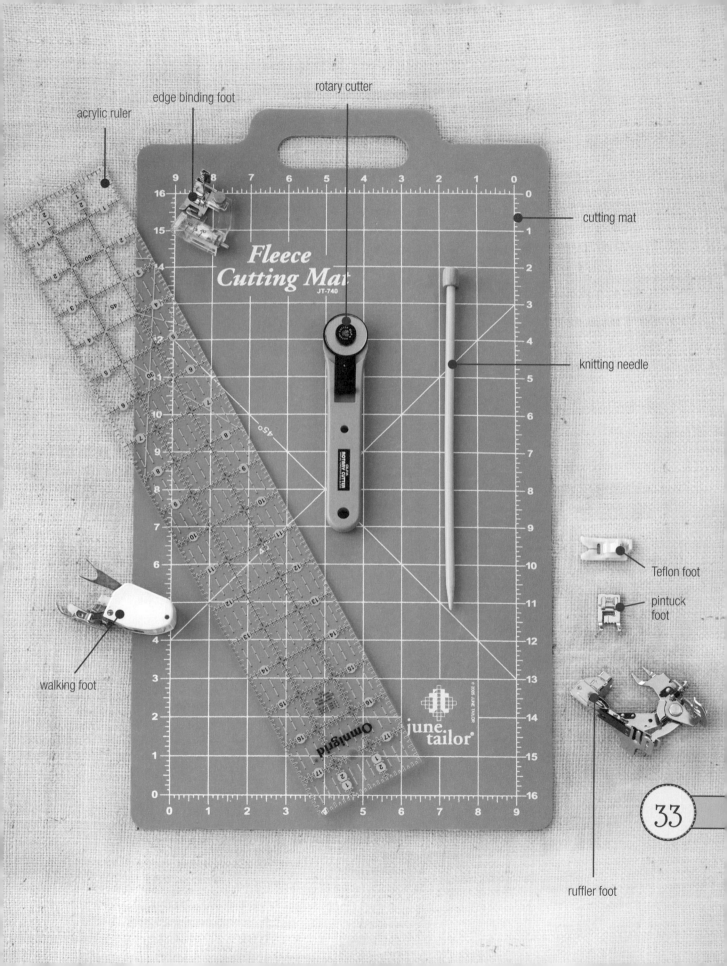

acrylic ruler

edge binding foot

rotary cutter

cutting mat

knitting needle

Teflon foot

pintuck foot

walking foot

ruffler foot

Fleece
Cutting Mat
JT-740

june.
tailor®

Omnigrid

33

GET 'EM IF YOU LIKE, BUT NO PRESSURE

NEEDLE THREADER

Threading a needle is one of those tasks that seems so daunting and impossible the first few times, that after a while becomes so habitual it's nearly reflexive. You'll end up threading your needle a lot, and anything that makes that job easier or faster is worth it. Needle threaders do that for you. Some sewing machines come with a needle threader attached, and folks who love them really, really love them. For hand sewing and embroidery, a handheld needle threader can be a lifesaver.

THIMBLE

Thimbles are so old-school they're nearly cliché, which is why I resisted getting one. I mean, aren't those for old ladies? They come in so many varieties, though, and if you've ever tried to jam a needle through layers of fabric and paid for your trouble, you've learned the value of a good thimble.

BIAS TAPE MAKER

Bias tape is one of my pet products, because I keep finding more and more uses for it. We'll talk a lot about bias tape in the next chapter and make some, too. When you make bias tape you fold under the edges on long strips of fabric. The bias tape maker does that for you. It has a wide end and a narrow end, with a curved side that forces the fabric strip into the right shape as it passes through. I use so much bias tape I don't know how I'd live without my gadget, but many people don't find it necessary. Bias tape makers come in sizes, and you choose based on how wide you want your finished tape to be.

EXPANDABLE MEASURE

I have a fantastic gadget that I got as a hand-me-down in a box of a zillion other things. I had no idea what it was but used it for years to mark the placement of pleats and to set buttonhole spacing. When I found the instruction sheet in another box ages later, I found I'd been using it for its intended purpose. If you're planning to do a lot of home decor (like piles of drapes), or if you expect to make blouse after buttoned blouse, I think an expandable measure, which is a type of hem guide, is a great investment. If you'll only ever make one buttoned shirt in your whole life, I'm pretty certain you can live without it.

NONSTICK PRESSING SHEET (NOT SHOWN)

My ironing board cover was a hot mess for many, many years—quite literally. Between scorching the fabric when the heat was too high and all the sticky press-on products I'd glued to the surface, I didn't think I'd ever have a cover that didn't look like it needed to be put out of its misery. And then I discovered nonstick pressing sheets. These thin sheets go under your project as you press to prevent getting interfacing or any other iron-on products all over your pretty cover.

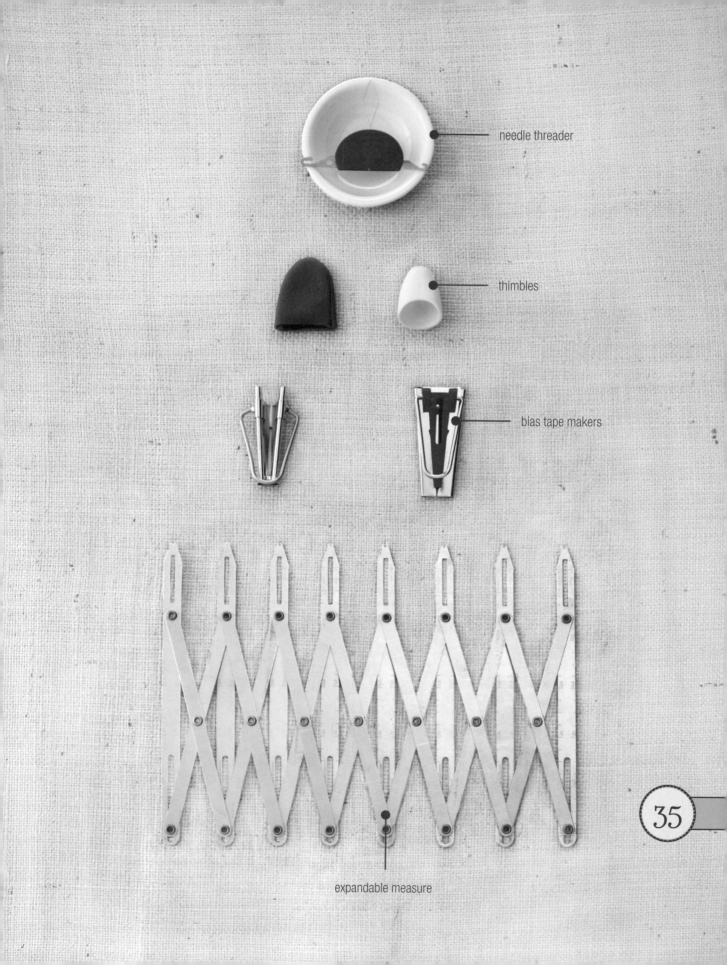

needle threader

thimbles

bias tape makers

expandable measure

35

PATTERN WEIGHTS

Pins are the usual way to hold your pattern to your fabric until you're ready to stitch it all together. In some cases, though, you might not want to use pins. Maybe you're working with a very fine fabric and don't want to damage it or leave holes. Maybe you're working with a slippery fabric, like rayon or satin, and pins would slide around and distort the fabric's shape. In these cases, pattern weights are a great option. They lie on top of the pattern and fabric and hold the pattern pieces in place as you mark and cut. They come in a variety of styles and sizes, so you can choose one that fits the project you're working on. And hey, if you don't have any on hand, canned goods or paperweights make great pattern weights!

IRONING HAM AND SEAM ROLL

Part of the world of clothing care that most of us have never experienced, the ironing ham and the seam roll are very 1950s, but so helpful for sewing. Both are very firmly stuffed, shaped pillows that allow you to mold your garment or project into just the right shape using the iron. Because these are smaller and more rounded than your ironing board, they allow you to get just the results you want. One side is a heavy cotton canvas for cotton fabrics, and the other is wool for pressing wool and winter fabrics.

SLEEVE BOARD

Like the ironing ham and seam roll, a sleeve board may look hopelessly outdated to you (me, I thought it was a dolly ironing board for the longest time). In truth, these puppies are sized and shaped in such a way that they allow you to access awkward parts of a project or garment with ease so you can get a good press and great results. They're also fantastic for pressing seams on smaller projects that won't fit over the end of your ironing board.

TUBE/LOOP TURNER

I mentioned in the last section that I like to use a knitting needle to turn things inside out, but they make actual products that do this for you, which are designed to work in even the tiniest spaces. Most tube or loop turners function by grasping one end of the fabric with a little hook, and holding onto it as the fabric is then pulled back through itself and turned to the right side. This can be great for belt loops and spaghetti straps—things that are at such a small scale that a knitting needle would never fit. In my experience, a lot of those hooks tend to shred my fabric, though, and because I never ever make spaghetti straps, I don't use one. If you're blessed with gorgeous shoulders and collarbones, though, and expect to make slinky dresses with spaghetti straps, a turner might just save your sanity.

TUBE PRESSING BAR

I suppose in some ways tube pressing bars are the companion gadget to the tube turners, but they're not the same thing. Some specialty embellishments, like Celtic appliqué, require long tubes of fabric to be pressed and stitched down to create shapes and designs. These little gizmos are the flat surface around which you can press your tubes to get the perfect shape. They also allow you to press seam allowances flat on really skinny stuff to ensure your work is top-notch. Basically, this is another item that's fun to have, but only if you're venturing into specialized territory.

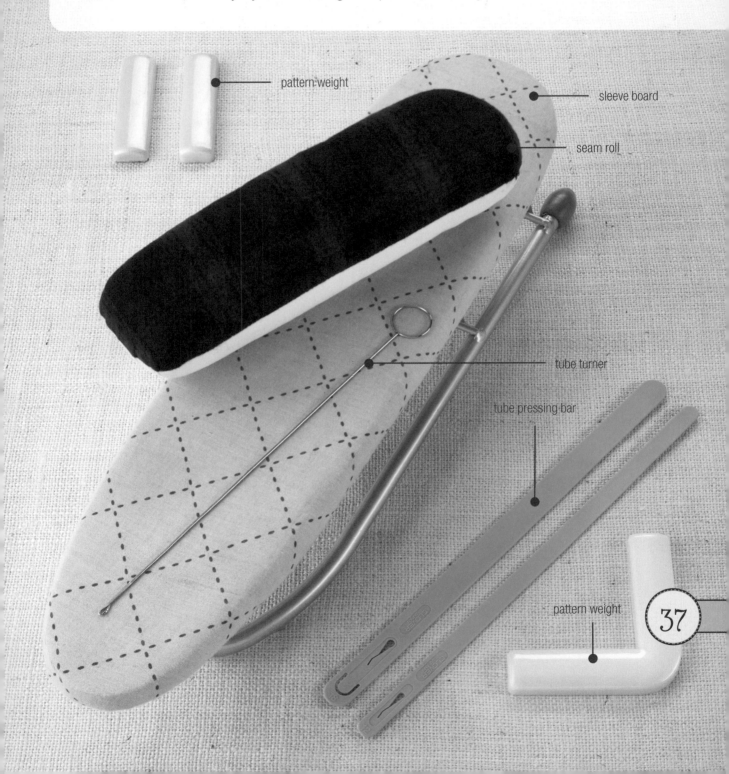

pattern weight

sleeve board

seam roll

tube turner

tube pressing bar

pattern weight

37

2

YOU AND YOUR MACHINE: A LOVE STORY

Given to me by my stepmother, my first sewing machine was a 1969 Singer, which weighed more than you and me put together. With a cast-iron construction and heavy-duty everything, it was an absolute beast. When I began sewing professionally, though, I knew I needed to invest in a newer model with some additional features. I purchased my current machine used and have never, ever regretted it: I was able to afford a lot more machine on my budget that way, and got all kinds of goodies thrown in at the same time. Today, I would go to bed with my sewing machine on the pillow next to me if I could, but my husband frowns on it.

I share this to indicate how attached you can get to your machine. Today, maybe you look out of the corner of your eye at a contraption you are certain will be your sworn enemy, but tomorrow you might feel a blossoming affection for your beast.

The first step in your relationship is getting to know one another.

CHOOSING A MACHINE

One of the most frequent questions I am asked is about how to choose the right sewing machine. It's a hard question to answer because, in some ways, which machine is right for you is subjective, and in others, it doesn't make a huge difference. The differences you'll see in most machines on the market are in how many and what types of functions they perform and in the interface.

Most people brand-new to sewing don't need a top-of-the-line quilting-and-embroidery machine; it's just a whole lot of machine to get to know, and so many are already intimidated by the mechanical-ness to begin with. More options are not necessarily better, especially if you never bother to use them. I know I might ruffle some feathers by saying this, but it's OK to get a starter machine to begin with, and then move up later once you really know you love sewing (which you totally will, FYI). Think of it like when you get your first place after moving away from home: Hardly anyone ever moves out and into a huge house with seven bedrooms and a chef's kitchen; most of us start with a small apartment and our own bathroom (oh, luxury!). Your first machine is kind of like that.

Now, I'm not advocating getting some junky little kiddie machine that won't work past the first week—far from it. There are several great models on the market that are reasonably priced, that will last you five or ten years and that you won't have to feel guilty passing on to someone else when you're ready to graduate to another, fancier machine (assuming you even do—some folks fall so in love with their starter machine that it's the only one they ever buy). You do want to look for some features, though, that will make your first machine great and help you avoid frustration:

- You'll want to be able to independently adjust the stitch length and stitch width. Some machines—usually the least expensive model manufactured by a particular brand—have preset stitch selections and don't allow you to adjust the length and width of your stitches by mixing and matching them. You really, really want to be able to do this.
- You want a machine that offers additional presser feet. At a minimum, look for a zipper foot and a buttonhole foot. More feet are nice but not necessary.
- Most machines offer you a free-arm feature, which allows you to remove a portion of the work area to make a smaller space that's more suitable for working on sleeves or cuffs. Steer clear of any machine where the work space is too wide to allow you to comfortably stitch smaller projects.

You'll notice that none of the features above precludes the purchase of a vintage machine. I've already waxed romantic about my 1969 Singer. Vintage machines can be fantastic finds and are often available for little or no money. Be sure to take it in to be serviced (any machine should see the doctor once a year for a regular check-up, just like you) so you'll know it's in good working condition before you get started. A good sewing machine shop also will give you some pointers on maintaining your machine at peak operating condition.

Beyond these basic guidelines, choosing a machine really becomes a matter of personal preference and aesthetics. Do you like the way it looks? Does it scare you with too many buttons? Do you prefer levers and dials to buttons and touchscreens when adjusting your settings? Sometimes the best way to make a decision is to go to a showroom and test drive a number of different models before making a commitment. My mom always taught me that if I left the store and didn't buy anything, the one I couldn't stop thinking about was the one I should go back and get (she was talking about pairs of shoes, but I think the advice holds true in this case, too). Do some test runs, go home and surf the Web to compare prices and features, and then jump in!

MACHINE PARTS

In the end, all sewing machines share certain traits in common, passed down from their forebears. The image on the next pages outlines the basics. Your particular model will have some variations, obviously, so use this guide in conjunction with your owner's manual to locate all the features you have at your disposal.

All sewing machines produced since the 1850s or so function in roughly the same way: An upper thread is carried by a needle through an opening where it loops around a lower thread before coming back up. When fabric is placed between the two threads, the loops bind the fabric together in the form of a stitch. Fancy, huh? Because little has changed in how sewing machines are constructed, a very basic schematic can be applied to almost all models.

Now's a good time, though, to point out some of the changes that have taken place in the last thirty years or so. When I demonstrate parts of the sewing machine to my classes, I use my 1969 Singer: It's made of cast iron, but it has all the same functions that the snazzy new machines do. It does have some features, though, that newer machines lack and that reveal a lot about how our image of who sews and what sewing should be has changed dramatically over the past few decades. First, it's made of cast iron, not high-grade heavy-duty plastic like nearly all newer machines. This machine was never intended to be portable (despite the fact that it was marketed that way at the time). It was manufactured in an era that had a number of assumptions about sewing: that every woman knew how to sew because someone somewhere had taught her; that every home had a sewing machine that got used on a regular basis; and that somewhere in that home was a place where that sewing machine was housed, like a sewing room or a nook in the kitchen. A heavy machine like this one didn't need to be carried around; it had a home. My ancient Singer has its motor and belt assembly on the outside of the machine, too, so that if the motor needed oil or the belt needed to be replaced, it could be accessed easily. Because, you know, you'd know how to do that. Last, the tension mechanism on this older model is external, unlike most newer machines, where it's all tucked away inside.

Demonstrating all these changes gives me a chance to think and talk about the ways that the structure of the machine is a reflection of who we are and who we want to be—like how tucking the motor inside to keep it from getting gummed up with dust reflects that many machines don't get used regularly or are stored in closets. I hope you'll look at your machine with compassion and a little affection after learning more about how it's made and what it can do!

1	SPOOL HOLDER	THROAT PLATE	9
2	THREAD GUIDES	FEED DOGS	10
3	TENSION MECHANISM	GUIDE LINES	11
4	TAKE-UP LEVER	PRESSER FOOT	12
5	THREAD GUIDES	PRESSER FOOT LEVER (in back; not visible in photo)	13
6	NEEDLE		
7	NEEDLE BAR	BOBBIN HOLDER	14
8	HANDWHEEL	BOBBIN WINDER	15

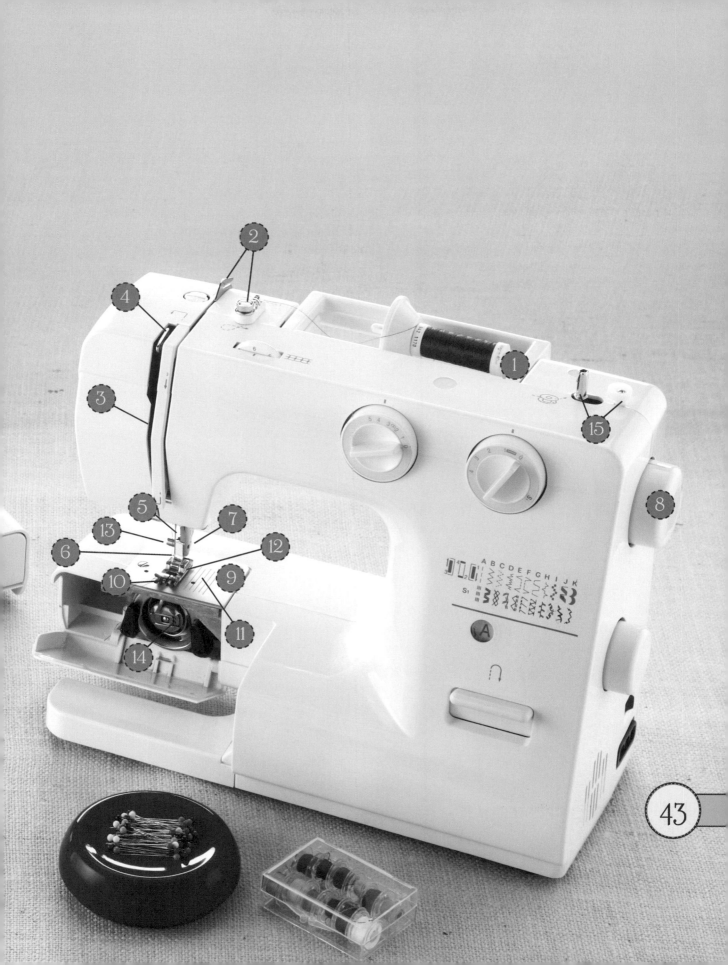

Let's walk through the process of threading your machine, and as we do, look at the functions of the various parts. Two birds, one stone. You'll find, too, that sewing terminology is delightfully uncomplicated in many cases, and the names of things are generally fairly clear indicators of their function.

THE UPPER THREADING

Start at the top of your machine, with the **spool holder (1)**. This is where the spool of thread will sit as you stitch. It may be vertical or horizontal; most horizontal models come with a cap of some kind to hold the spool in place so it doesn't go spinning off into the distance as your machine picks up speed.

From there, your thread will travel through one or more **thread guides (2)** These serve to carry the thread so it doesn't get tangled through the machine's innards.

The thread guides will lead you past the machine's **tension mechanism (3)**. (We'll talk more about tension at the end of the chapter; it's very important.)

After the tension mechanism, you'll run the thread through the **take-up lever (4)**. It does just what it sounds like: carries the thread up and down as the machine creates stitches.

Below the take-up lever you'll find one or more **thread guides (5)**, and finally the **needle (6)**, which on most newer models threads front-to-back (some older models, especially Singers, thread side-to-side). Voila, you're done!

THE PRESSER FOOT AND THROAT PLATE

So, here we are at the needle, where all the action is. You can see that the needle is inserted in the **needle bar (7)**, which raises and lowers as the motor turns the **handwheel (8)**. Give it a test: Turn your handwheel toward you (toward you because that's how the motor works) and watch as the take-up lever and the needle move up and down.

As the needle descends, it disappears into a hole in a metal plate, called the **throat plate (9)**. This plate has a number of openings, one that allows the needle to go beneath it, and two others that have rows of sharp teeth peeking out. Turn that handwheel again, and you'll see that as the needle goes up and down, the teeth—called **feed dogs (10)**—move to the back, drop down, come forward, lift up, and move to the back again, over and over. This action moves your fabric through the machine. Using a sewing machine isn't like Fred Flintstone driving: You don't have to move the fabric through yourself. The feed dogs do that for you.

Stitch Tip

Did you know that you can lower your feed dogs and still sew? Sure! Maybe you want to sew your buttons on with the machine or use your thread to create artful drawings. Look either on the back of the machine or next to the bobbin case; many newer machines have a lever that will allow you to drop the feed dogs and take some real control.

Surrounding the feed dogs on the throat plate is a series of **guide lines (11)**, score marks in the metal of the plate. Each of these lines represents the distance from the needle and is how we maintain a straight stitch line while sewing. The standard measurement in the U.S. is eighths of an inch, so each of those score marks indicates distance from the needle in those increments. The first one isn't ⅛" (3.2mm), though, since the presser foot is between the needle and the line. Use your seam gauge or a ruler to determine which line is which: you especially want to identify ⅜" (1 cm) and ⅝" (1.6cm) since these are the most common seam allowances in sewing. Some folks like to lay down a piece of masking or painter's tape at ⅝" (1.6cm) as an easy guide while working. You can also attach your seam guide (see page 24) here.

I've mentioned the **presser foot (12)** several times now. That's the flat-bottomed ski-like part through which the needle passes. The presser foot is squeezed down on top of the feed dogs when it's lowered by the **presser foot lever (13)**, usually on the back or inside arm of the machine. The fabric goes between the presser foot and the feed dogs, and as the feed dogs move the fabric forward, the presser foot keeps it from flying all over the place. The most common rookie mistake I see is leaving the presser foot up when beginning to stitch—things will go all kinds of wrong, and it's a mistake you won't make more than once!

Your sewing machine operates by using two threads: the upper thread and the bobbin thread. A bobbin is a small spool that fits in the **bobbin holder (14)** below the throat plate and allows the top thread to make a loop in your fabric—that loop is a stitch. To use the bobbin, you'll first have to wind it. Prewound bobbins are sold at some sewing stores but generally contain inferior quality thread and are for emergency purposes only (and probably not even then).

On top of your machine is a little gizmo I call a "bobbin nobbin." This is the **bobbin winder (15)**, which will hold the bobbin and rotate it while it winds thread off your spool. (Turn the page to find out exactly how to wind the bobbin.)

POWER AND LIGHT

To run the motor, you have a foot pedal, which attaches to the machine via a cord. Your pedal should be turned so that the angle is going up, away from you, like a ramp or like the gas pedal in your car (rather than with the ramp down toward you, which gives you significantly less control over your speed and acceleration). Near the port where the foot pedal connects, you'll find a power switch—if your machine isn't working, check here first! Most power switches also activate a small light over the throat plate that illuminates the work area. In older machines, the circuit from lightbulb to motor is often a direct one, meaning that if the lightbulb blows, the machine won't run.

Technique
WINDING THE BOBBIN

1. INSERT THREAD IN BOBBIN

Insert the spool of thread onto the spool holder. Then place the end of your thread coming off the spool (don't cut the thread—go straight from the spool) through one of the holes in the side of the bobbin. Do this from the inside.

2. HAND-WIND THREAD

Hand-wind the thread around the bobbin a few times, just to get it jump-started. We'll finish this with the power of the motor, but starting it by hand gives it a headstart and makes for better results.

3. POP BOBBIN IN PLACE

Now take the bobbin to the bobbin winder and place it on the winder so the thread end comes off the bobbin at the top. The winder will rotate clockwise, so you want to be sure the bobbin is placed with the thread wound in that direction. Press the bobbin into place until it clicks.

4. THREAD AND LET BOBBIN WIND

You should have at least one thread guide on the top of the machine that guides the thread between the spool and the bobbin; on most machines, that thread will cross over itself and form an X—this makes a better-wound bobbin.

Hit the gas and watch the bobbin go! Your machine will stop winding automatically when the bobbin is full. Cut the thread and remove the bobbin from the bobbin winder.

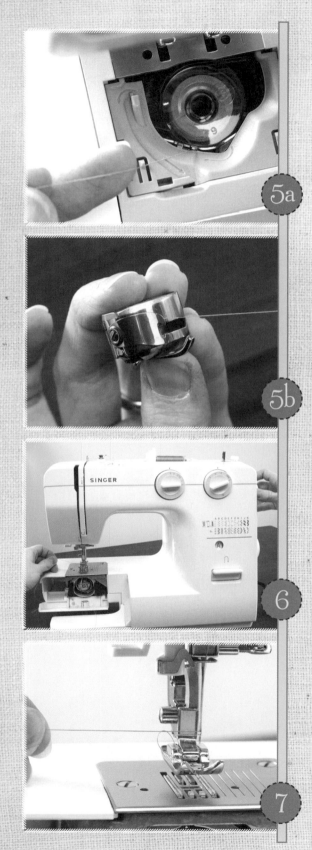

5. INSERT BOBBIN IN CASE

OPTION A: DROP-IN

Most newer machines have a drop-in bobbin. Place your bobbin in the case and take the thread through the channel at the bottom. There will be a teeny opening through which the thread should pass—this is the tension mechanism for the bobbin, and getting the thread in place here is essential to getting good stitches.

OPTION B: VERTICAL

Older machines—and some newer ones—use a bobbin case that inserts into the machine vertically and holds the bobbin in position. If your machine has one of these, place the bobbin inside the case and bring the thread through the metal opening in the side until it emerges from the small hole. Ensure that the needle is in the highest position, then line up the finger on the bobbin case with the matching indentation on the interior of the machine to get a good lock. The bobbin case should be firmly in place and shouldn't come out if you give it a little wiggle.

6. BRING THREAD UP

Before moving on, thread your machine (as you learned on pages 44–45). Next, bring the bobbin thread up, which you have to do before you can do any sewing. Take the top thread in your left hand and hold it steady. Place your right hand on the handwheel and turn it one full rotation so the needle goes down into the throat plate and comes back up a single time. As it does that, you'll see it pass by the bobbin and grab that bobbin thread: You've made a stitch!

7. PULL LOOP AND FINISH

When the needle comes back to the top position, tug on the thread in your left hand until a loop appears. Pull that loop to the top, and your bobbin thread is up. Take both threads and move them under the presser foot and toward the back of the machine—this will prevent you from sewing back over them and worrying that you've made a mistake when you haven't.

NEEDLES: WHAT YOU NEED TO KNOW

After you learn to thread your machine, you start to see that a lot of your sewing revolves around your needle. A needle is a needle is a needle, right? Well, not entirely. Needles should be suited to the fabric you'll be stitching. Different needles have different styles of points, and each style of point is best used for a particular fabric.

Sharp needles are designed to pierce the fibers of woven fabrics. The point is exceptionally sharp to make a clean hole at the point of entry. Different gauges of needle are suited to different weights of fabric—larger needles for heavier fabrics, smaller needles for more delicate fabrics.

A type of sharp needle, **universal points** are slightly rounded so they can be used on a wide range of fabrics.

Ballpoint needles are rounded to allow the tip to push aside the fibers of knit fabrics. Sharp needles will snag on knits and cause them to bunch and ravel. To stitch knit fabrics, you'll want ballpoint needles.

In addition to the sharpness of the point on your needle, be aware that needles come in sizes. Smaller needles have smaller numbers, and smaller needles are suitable for finer fabrics. A 9, then, is better for silks while a 14 is best used on denim or canvas.

BASIC STITCHING

Stitching is, of course, central to sewing. Now that you know your machine and have learned how to thread it, let's talk about actually using it!

The Seam Allowance

When the fabric is set in the machine, the distance between the cut edge of the fabric and the needle is called the seam allowance. It's the little bit of extra fabric that gives your stitches something to bite into. The industry standard seam allowance in the U.S. is ⅝" (1.6cm), a ridiculously wasteful seam allowance, if you ask me. It's the one you'll find on almost all published patterns, though, so we'll use it in some of the projects. To figure out how much is a ⅝" (1.6cm) seam allowance (or any other seam allowance measure), check the guide lines on the throat plate. Place the fabric with the cut edge alongside the guide line that represents the seam allowance measurement.

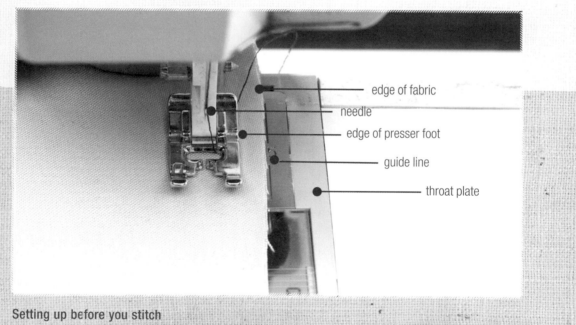

edge of fabric
needle
edge of presser foot
guide line
throat plate

Setting up before you stitch

This photo shows how to use the guide lines on the throat plate. Now you can see why taking your time to get straight cuts will pay off when it comes time to stitch.

Stitch Tip

If you need a guide for a ¼" (6.4mm) seam allowance, look no farther than your presser foot. For most sewing machine models, the right edge of the presser foot is about ¼" (6.4mm) from the needle.

Straight Stitches: The Driver's Ed Theory

When I took driver's ed, our instructor told us we should always be looking twelve car lengths in front of us as we drive. Now, when you're fifteen, that's about the dumbest advice you've ever heard, but it totally works: Looking at the steering wheel does nothing to improve your driving, right? The same is true of sewing. Your instinct will likely be to look at the needle, but that needle is going to do what it's going to do whether you're looking at it or not. Instead, keep your eyes on the throat plate. Your goal is to watch the relationship between the cut edge of the fabric and the score mark on the throat plate—keep that consistent, and your stitches will be, too.

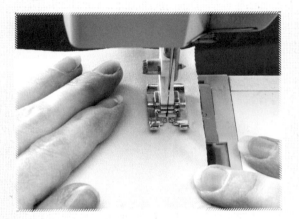

GUIDELINES FOR STITCHING STRAIGHT
Begin with the needle in the fabric and the presser foot down. (If you begin with the needle up, the thread tends to want to jump out of the needle.) From here, start stitching. Your goal is to maintain a consistent relationship between the edge of the fabric and the seam guide on the throat plate: Place your hands on either side of the fabric (or in front and back, if you prefer, remembering not to tug or pull as the fabric goes under the presser foot) and simply steer the fabric to keep it on the guideline.

Length, Width and Variations

The default or regular stitch length is usually set at a length of 2.5 or so, and a width of zero (a straight stitch). Stitch length, ultimately, is the frequency with which the needle pierces the fabric. A short stitch length means the needle is going in and out of the fabric very often, and a long one means the machine is pulling lots of fabric through between each needle puncture. In your stitch sampler (on the next page) you'll play with adjusting the width as you sew. (A good machine will let you mix-and-match length and width to achieve almost limitless combinations.) You'll also try out specialty stitches your machine will allow you to make. Here's a highlight of some of the most useful:

- ✺ **Zigzag stitch:** used for finishing edges, for working with stretchy fabrics, for decorative stitching and machine appliqué (see page 57!).
- ✺ **Buttonhole stitch:** just what it sounds like—a stitch that allows you to make buttonholes. Some machines, mostly older ones, don't have one. Newer machines usually have a special setting and a presser foot for buttonholes.
- ✺ **Blind hem stitch:** a stitch that allows you to create a nearly invisible hem. It involves some fancy folding, but it's a cool skill to have.
- ✺ **Stretch stitch:** intended for knits. Using a standard stitch on knits doesn't give the necessary stretch and will result in broken threads. The stretch stitch avoids that by working with the give of the knit fabric to move when the fabric does.

Mini-Project
STITCH SAMPLER

The best way to find out what you and your machine can do is to put it through its paces, so here's a real project for you to try! For most of American history, women have created stitch samplers to demonstrate their skill with the needle. The majority of the samplers we have available—many of them housed at the Smithsonian—are representatives of hand sewing, such as cross-stitch and embroidery. The concept of creating a sampler holds true for machine stitching as well: The best way to learn how to create the stitches you want to use is to practice making them. As you create your stitch sampler, you'll learn more essentials of stitching, like backtacking and setting your stitch length.

shopping list + supplies

Basic Sewing Tools (see page 23)

½ yard (46cm) of solid quilt-weight cotton fabric (or muslin)

contrasting thread

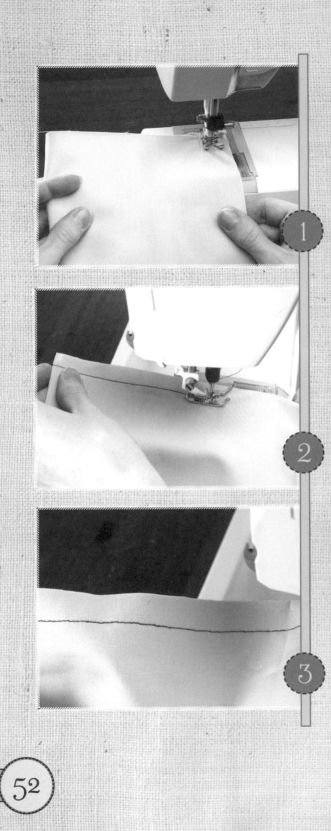

1. FOLD FABRIC AND PLACE ON MACHINE

Fold the fabric in half lengthwise so it is doubled and measures about 18" × 22" (46cm × 56cm). Doubling the fabric makes it slightly more substantial and will give your stitches something to bite into as you practice. Place the fabric on your machine with the open edges on your right and the folded edge on your left. Set the fabric for a ⅝" (1.6cm) seam allowance and lower the presser foot.

2. SET STITCH LENGTH AND STITCH

Many newer machines are computerized and have an automated default stitch length that appears when the machine is turned on. Other machines are electronic but not computerized: Their stitches are adjusted manually. Regardless of which your machine is, set the machine to what will likely be your all-the-time stitch length (2.5), just to get used to it. So put the stitch width at zero, for a straight stitch (no side-to-side movement) and the stitch length at 2.5. Stitch a straight line for about 5" (13cm) or so.

3. CHANGE STITCH LENGTH

Now let's mix it up a bit: Make the stitch length shorter (less than 2.5) and stitch for a bit. See how much closer together the stitches are? After that, extend the stitch length (greater than 2.5) and see how much farther apart they are. Finish this first row with your longest stitch length.

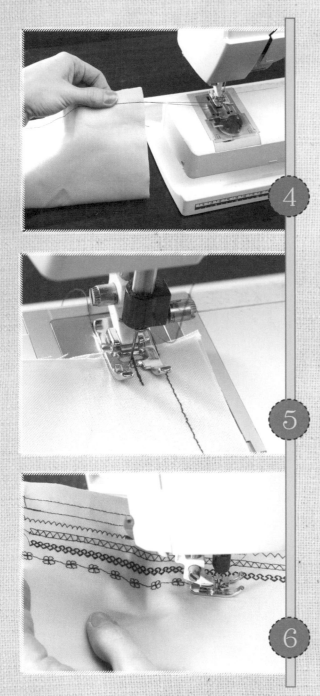

4. REMOVE WORK FROM MACHINE

When the row is done, make sure the needle is in its highest postition, lift your presser foot and pull the fabric away from the machine, out to the left. If your machine resists this, or if you see more than two threads attached to the machine, try turning your handwheel another half turn. Often, if the needle isn't raised all the way, an unfinished stitch will get stuck in the bobbin case and make you think you've made some horrible mistake, when it's a simple fix. Trim the threads close to the project rather than close to the machine so you won't need to rethread before you begin the next row.

5. RUN NEW ROW WITH BACKTACKING

If you take the ends of the fabrics you just stitched together and pull just a bit, you'll see how easily they come apart. Backtacking (also commonly called backstitching) is a technique that locks your stitches in place and keeps them from unraveling. For almost all sets of stitches, you need to backtack when you start a row and then backtack when you finish.

Run a second row of straight stitches next to the first. As a guide, use the edge of the presser foot as it runs up against the first row of stitches. When you run this second row, backtack at both ends. To backtack, take two or three stitches forward, and then hold down your reverse button and take two or three stitches back, and then release the reverse button and stitch forward along the rest of the seam. When you reach the end of your seam, stop and press the reverse button, take two or three stitches back, then two or three stitches forward.

6. COMPLETE SAMPLER

For the rest of the sampler, continue to run rows of stitches. Begin with a row of zigzag stitches. This means you'll set your stitch length at 2.5 and adjust your stitch width. Like the last rows, feel free to stitch for a bit, stop, adjust the width, and begin again until you've played with all the widths. (Width is how far right and left of center the needle jumps, and is the basis for all your specialty stitches.)

Then take some time to experiment with any specialty stitches you have on your machine. You can adjust the type of stitch by selecting it from the knob or menu on the front of the machine, and then simply run a row parallel to the previous stitches, using the edge of your presser foot as a guide.

Stitch Tip

Get in the habit of always backtacking so you'll know your seams are nice and secure. Unless otherwise indicated, you will need to backtack at the beginning and end of each set of stitches for the projects in this book.

Curved Stitches: How to Stay on the Road

Stitching curved edges is very much like stitching straight lines in that your goal is to maintain a steady, consistent seam allowance. It can be more challenging at first to keep the edge from swinging too wide or from getting too close to the needle as you move into the turn—in the same way that when you first learn to drive a car it can be hard to know when to brake going into a curve and when to accelerate coming out of it.

STITCHING A CONCAVE CURVE

When stitching a concave, or inward, curve, guide the fabric toward the machine as it passes under the presser foot. Do this with gentle pressure on the back end of the fabric, allowing you to keep a steady, even seam allowance.

STITCHING A CONVEX CURVE

When stitching a convex, or outward, curve, guide the fabric away from the machine as it passes under the presser foot. Do this with gentle pressure on the back of the fabric and keep your eyes on the seam guide to keep your distance clean and even.

Stitch Tip

On the book CD you will find stitch guides for practicing straight and curved stitching.

Mini-Project THREAD DRAWING

Remember when I mentioned (on page 44) that you can lower your feed dogs? Here's the arty application of that function. (If you can't lower your feed dogs, you can still do this mini-project.) You're about to use your newfound knowledge of stitching straight lines and curves to thread draw and create thread art! What I love about thread drawing is the limitless possibility: Sketch an original drawing or recreate a masterpiece by one of the great painters—anything you like!

shopping list + supplies

Basic Sewing Tools (see page 23)

piece of solid quilt-weight cotton fabric (or muslin)

marking chalk

contrasting thread (in multiple colors, if desired)

1. DRAW PATTERN

Start by drawing a simple picture with the marking chalk. You can do something really simple, like a cloud, or more involved. I drew several flowers with different petals and leaves.

2. STITCH

Lower the feed dogs on your machine (if you're able). Then trace your chalk drawing with machine stitching. Beyond that, there are no rules! You can camp out in one spot and apply a lot of thread there. You can also move very quickly past another and place hardly any thread there. The amount of thread you stitch will create a variety of looks for your design.

Stitch Tip

This project is all about practicing with freedom. So feel free to swap out colors and vary your stitch length. Want to try a specialty stitch? Have at it! As long you're stitching, you're good to go.

POWER PHRASE #1

66 YOU'RE THE BOSS! 99
(NOT TONY DANZA—YOU)

Don't let that machine sass you, or make you feel like you can't do this. You can. That's just a machine, and you're in charge! Be the boss.

Mini-Project MACHINE-APPLIQUÉ TEE

Now that you've had free rein, it's time to get down to business and really practice those straight and curved stitches. Let's try a simple project that has so many variations it'll make you feel like a rock star right out of the gate.

Appliqué is an old technique, usually done by hand. It's gotten a bit of a bad rap over the years as being stodgy and too traditional, but modern crafters have been doing some amazing things with the technique. It can be time-consuming, but the results are often stunning and quite artful. For quicker results, though, you can appliqué using your machine. Instead of turning edges of fabric shapes under by hand, appliqué by machine allows you to finish the edges using your zigzag stitch, simultaneously securing them to the fabric and preventing the edges from unraveling.

shopping list + supplies

Basic Sewing Tools
(see page 23)

T-shirt

fusible webbing

scrap of fabric

stabilizer

matching thread

1. FUSE WEBBING TO FABRIC

You'll be using fusible webbing to create a fabric "sticker" for the appliqué shape. The webbing (which is sold under brand names like WonderUnder and Heat'n Bond) is a heat-activated two-sided glue that allows you to position your shape on the fabric to which it will be attached, and then prevents it from shifting as you stitch.

Place the scrap of fabric right side down on the ironing board. With the webbing sticky side down, place the fusible webbing on the wrong side of the fabric. Apply heat and pressure according to the instructions (each brand has slightly different requirements).

2. CUT OUT SHAPE

With the paper backing still in place, draw your shape. For this project, I used a deceptively simple shape: a heart.

I recommend a heart first because it's simple, but still has both straight lines and curves. (For appliqué projects, almost anything is possible—the world is your oyster! Oooh, hey, how about an oyster?) Cut out the shape along the lines you've drawn.

3. PEEL OFF BACKING

When you're ready to place your shape on the shirt, peel off the paper backing and position your new fabric sticker on the shirt where you'd like to have it stitched down.

Stitch Tip

You can layer multiple shapes to create an interesting design. If you do that, keep in mind that shapes that will be on the bottom really ought to be stitched first, followed by the other shapes layered on top of them. If this sounds intimidating or like more work than you are interested in doing, no problem! You can simply throw all the shapes down at one time and stitch away, adjusting when necessary. This is supposed to be fun, after all.

4. BOND SHAPE TO FABRIC

The shape is bonded to the fabric with heat. Simply press it according to the manufacturer's instructions and allow it to cool.

5. ADD STABILIZER

Knits have special requirements. If you've ever tried to stitch on a T-shirt before, you know that they can bunch and shift as they go under the presser foot and create a real nightmare. Using a stabilizer prevents the shirt from moving around and gets you much better results.

Stabilizer is another heat-activated product. It allows you to secure the fabric in position before stitching to make sure it doesn't shift or move about and spoil your design. With paper side up and glossy side down press the stabilizer to the inside of the shirt, making sure that you've covered the back of the shape you placed on the front. Any section where you stitch without stabilizer is likely to snag.

6. SET PROJECT IN MACHINE

Place the project under the needle. I usually put the shirt inside out, and work from the right side. That way, I don't have to worry that I'll accidentally stitch the front of the shirt to the back and then have to rip it all out later. Line up the edge of your appliqué with the center of the needle, so that as you stitch, your needle will go on and off the edge of the appliqué fabric, covering all of those raw edges in thread. This will prevent the edge from unraveling when you launder your project later.

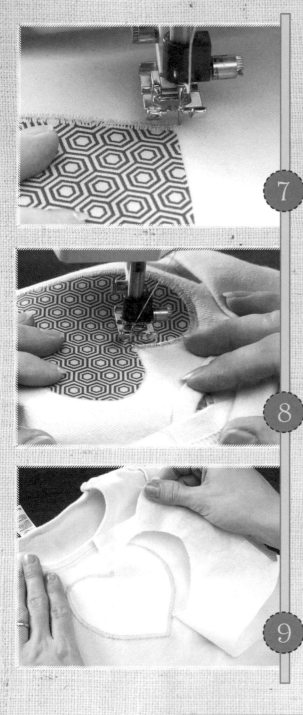

7. SET STITCHES AND START SEWING

Now comes the fun part: stitching it all down. You'll be using the zigzag stitch, so change your stitch width to the widest stitch setting your machine allows. Then set your stitch length to a very short stitch, usually between zero and one. This combination of a zigzag and a super-short stitch length is called satin stitch.

(Some machines don't allow you to independently adjust your stitch length and width; they give you preset stitches instead. If that's the case for you, look for the stitch on your machine that allows you to get the shortest zigzag possible.)

Now, start stitching down the straight part of the heart. When you get to the point, stitch beyond the tip of the point for a couple of stitches and then pivot with the needle in the fabric. When you turn, your new stitches will cover the previous ones and make them an invisible part of the whole.

8. STITCH CURVES

Stitching the curves is a little trickier, so take it slowly and follow the curve as closely as you can. For the the divot at the top of the heart, stop your stitches shortly before you get to the point, and then pivot with the needle in your fabric. When you turn, the new stitches will cover the section you left unstitched.

9. REMOVE STABILIZER

After the entire design is stitched down, remove the shirt from the machine. Remove the stabilizer from the inside and trim your threads.

Don't you feel powerful with all the potential designs appliqué offers you right at your fingertips?

Alternate Stitches for Appliqué

Machine appliqué doesn't always have to be done with satin stitch. Using a simple zigzag does the same job—it keeps the edges of your appliqué fabric from fraying—but has a more casual, devil-may-care attitude about it. You can even use a straight stitch inside the edge to perform the same function, and then enjoy the slightly fuzzy finish as those unstitched edges fray slightly wash after wash.

TENSION: YOURS AND YOUR MACHINE'S

The tension assembly on your sewing machine is housed within the machine's interior, so on most newer models, you can't really see what's going on in there. On older models, you'll see that tension is controlled by a knob and that the thread interacts with that knob in some mysterious way as you sew. Let's uncloak the mystery, and head off some questions about tension while you're at it.

First, when I talk about tension, I'm really talking about the tension placed on the thread as it makes its way to the needle. That tension is created by a pair of disks in some machines, by springs in others: When tension is increased on the machine's settings, it releases less thread to get to the needle, and when tension is decreased on the machine's settings, it releases more thread to get to the needle.

Often when you run into tension problems, the issue isn't the setting but the way the thread is sitting in those tension disks. Your default solution should be to unthread the machine—just pull the whole spool all the way off—and rethread from scratch. Most of the time, this will make it all better. If not, it might very well be the tension setting. Try the tips below to diagnose the issue and set things right.

Common Tension Problems: Troubleshooting

Too much tension

If the tension on your upper thread is set too high, it will yank the bobbin thread back up through the fabric and create "pops" on top of your project. Correct by decreasing your tension setting.

Not enough tension

If the tension on the upper thread is too loose, the bobbin thread will pull it through to the bottom and create a giant nasty mess. You'll think you've ruined your machine, and your project, and you'll be tempted to despair. Fear not! First, check the thread take-up lever. Did the thread jump ship when you weren't watching? This is the most likely culprit; even a little vibration from the table you're working on can cause the thread to move out of place, creating a tension issue.

61

3

FABRIC: A PRIMER

As a openly greedy fabric junkie, I've played with a lot of fabric. Like many others, I've been guilty of purchasing fabric just to hold it; buying yards and yards and yards and having no idea what I'll do with it; and keeping bits of really good stuff for years. I used to go to the fabric store and buy a half yard or a yard, until I learned that I never had enough on hand when I decided to use that particular piece of fabric. So I began buying two yards at a time. Then three yards. Then I began to say, "I'll take whatever is left on the bolt." My husband wondered where it was all going to go, but I simply washed and folded and admired and re-folded and was deaf to his cries. I do not apologize for this behavior.

For many, fabric is what gets them started sewing: the sheer potential, the absolute possibility of it all. What leads to disappointment, though, is when fabric and pattern are married poorly, and they create a final product that falls short of their dreams. Knowing something about how fabric is made and anticipating how it will behave is your best defense against this travesty. Let's spend some time going over the basics that will help you have the most success with your projects right out of the gate. I don't claim to cover everything there is to know about fabric, or every type of fabric out there, but we'll touch on the issues you'll confront most, and the fabrics you'll lust after first.

SO YOU'RE IN THE FABRIC STORE...

Even if you've been in the fabric store dozens of times, it can be super confusing to figure out which fabrics do what and how to choose the perfect one for your project. Let's do a lap around the shop before we commit to a location, and evaluate what's out there.

45" Verus 60" Bolts, Home Decor versus Apparel, Help!

First of all, most fabrics come either double-rolled on a cardboard bolt or rolled on a tube. What you'll be most accustomed to, if you are looking for fabrics for apparel or crafts, is a double-rolled bolt. These fabrics are either 45" (1.1m) wide or 60" (1.5m) wide. Because they're folded in half, they're stored on either a 22" (56cm) bolt (for 45" [1.1m] fabrics) or a 29" (74cm) bolt (for 60" [1.5m] fabrics). Many of these fabrics are categorized as quilt-weight cottons, but most fabrics are flexible and can be used for crafts and apparel with equal success.

Fabrics that are especially heavy, like upholstery-weight cottons, or fabrics that are especially light, like drapery sheers, are usually rolled on the tube. This prevents them from being folded in half, which would inevitably leave a permanent crease; since you're unlikely to launder upholstery fabrics or sheers, rolling them flat is the ideal way to store them prior to use. Most fabrics rolled on a tube measure 55"–60" (1.4m–1.5m) wide, although it's not uncommon to see upholstery fabrics that are 72" (1.8m) wide or more.

Natural Versus Man-Made Fibers

When you sew, your hands are in direct contact with the fabric you've selected. Even when you wear a garment, you won't touch the fabric as often as when you sew with it. For that reason, I vastly prefer working with natural fibers. Cotton, wool, linen, bamboo and silk all feel delicious beneath your fingers, and each has a predictable drape and behavior that allows you to choose just the right fabric for your project. Polyester and polyester blends, by definition, contain man-made fibers—that is to say, they're partly made of spun plastic.

Does that mean you can never work with blends? Goodness, no. Even I make an exception for rayon, which is an affordable alternative to silk, and I like a nice Tencel blend here and there. (Tencel is a fabric made from recycled wood pulp fibers.) But be aware of what you're buying and how it will behave.

Natural fibers are much less likely to pill and wear out, and will stay nice longer than any man-made option. Higher quality supplies mean higher quality results almost every time.

COTTON

WOOL

SILK

DOUBLE GAUZE

PIQUE

VOILE

CANVAS

CORDUROY

LINEN

HOW FABRIC IS MADE

Modern looms use thousands upon thousands of threads woven together to create fabric. This weaving process dictates the behavior of fabric and how it responds to our attempts to cut and shape it.

Looms are preloaded with fibers running top to bottom—north to south, if you will. These are the warp threads and are the strongest and most firmly tied of the threads in your woven fabric. Perpendicular to these and woven over and under them are the weft threads, which are slightly looser, and wrap around the warp threads on each side of the fabric.

Weave

A fabric's weave is a reference to how the threads are strung on the loom when it's woven. How the threads relate to one another determines what the fabric looks like, how well it wears and how heavy it is.

PLAIN

Plain weave is the most common and the weave with which you are likely the most familiar. When plain-weave fabrics are created, the weft threads go over and under each successive thread in the fabric, never skipping a thread. It's a simple technique that creates a smooth fabric with a gentle drape. Quilt-weight cotton fabric is an example of plain weave.

TWILL

Twill weave involves the weft threads wrapping under two warp threads, then one, then two, then one, and on and on, creating a slight diagonal pattern in the fabric and giving it slightly greater strength. This weave is what you see in chinos and denim.

SATIN

Satin weave is the third most common weave you'll run across. Most of us hear "satin" and think specifically of prom or wedding dresses. But in fact, the term *satin* refers to how the fabric is made: The silky texture is the result of having four or more warp threads beneath each weft thread that crosses it. This makes a super smooth fabric that's a joy to touch—but a little harder to work with than the trusty plain weave.

Pattern and Print

Printed fabrics are exactly what they sound like: They are solid-colored (usually white) fabrics that have been screen-printed with a design in ink. As you look at a print, consider the way it is laid out on the fabric. Prints can be all over the place or have a top and bottom. This is referred to as the direction of the print, and it has an impact on how and where you place your pattern pieces to cut out. When you're using a solid-colored fabric, it doesn't really make much difference if you turn a pattern piece upside down to make your whole pattern fit. When you have a print, it might, though, and that affects how much fabric you'll need to buy.

TOSSED PRINT

A tossed print is one in which the images are every which way, and you're free to rotate the fabric a full 360 degrees without finding anything upside down. These are easy prints to work with and very common. Most florals are tossed prints. Four-way directionals are similar to tossed prints: they can be flipped 180 or 90 degrees, but not another angle, and still be the same print.

ONE-WAY DIRECTIONALS

One-way prints, as you probably guessed, have images that only go one way. Many are obvious: they're usually faces or letters or trees or other real-world objects that have clear tops and bottoms. When cutting, be careful to recognize that flipping a pattern piece over to save space might result in Elvis's head pointing at your feet.

TWO-WAY DIRECTIONALS

A two-way print can be rotated 180 degrees but not 90. The images are the same upside down, but not side to side. A stripe is a two-way print.

Nap

Like printed fabrics, some solid fabrics have a direction. Corduroy, velvet and chenille are all examples of this: If you brush your hand in one direction, the fabric is rough and in the other it's smooth. This is referred to as nap. Most commercial sewing patterns will refer to laying out your pattern pieces "with nap" and "without nap." This is a reference to the fact that fabrics with a one-way print or a texture will require more fabric to ensure that the pattern pieces are all going in the correct direction. Nap on corduroy should be going down (should feel smooth when you brush your hand down it) and on velvet should be going up (to catch the light and give the fabric the proper complexity and depth).

Selvage, Grainline and Bias

When woven fabric comes off the loom at the mill, it has some very specific properties. Not to sound too science-y, but without a basic knowledge of these properties, a lot of sewing lingo will be lost on you. It's best to go over some details now so the terms you'll be hearing for, you know, the rest of your sewing life will be meaningful to you.

grainline

bias

crossgrain

Nature-ology by STUDIO E fabrics · www.studioefabrics.com ① ○ ③

selvage edge

SELVAGE

When fabric is woven, the weft threads must wrap around the warp threads at each side of the fabric as it passes through the loom. As they do, they make a finished edge that won't unravel and is tightly woven. This is called the selvage (or selvedge) edge. What's great about the selvage is that it's a nice, straight line. What's stinky about it is that because it's woven tightly, it shrinks at a different rate than the rest of your fabric, and so should be removed prior to working with your yardage. We'll talk a bit more about how to do this properly in the next chapter.

GRAINLINE

Grainline is an important term in sewing. It refers to all the threads in your woven fabric that are parallel to the selvage, which is to say, all the warp threads. This is where your fabric has the least give and is most tightly woven. Because the weave is more snug here, your fabric will distort the least as a result of gravity. All commercial patterns include an indicator of how to orient your pattern pieces in relation to the grainline, so knowing how to find it is a huge skill.

CROSSGRAIN

Just like the term implies, the crossgrain goes across the grainline. It's found in the threads that are perpendicular to the grainline, so, in the weft threads. This is where your fabric has a little more give and flexibility as a result of the weaving process. Some patterns allow you to orient pattern pieces along the crossgrain to take advantage of a border print, for example.

BIAS

If you fold the selvage edge of a cut of fabric so it lies along the crossgrain (and creates a little triangle at the corner), the hypotenuse of that triangle is called the bias line of the fabric. In this case, bias means the same as it does in journalism: it's an angle, a bent. This 45-degree angle cuts right along the diagonal between your warp and weft threads, and represents the line along which your fabric has the most give and stretch. On page 72, you'll learn to create continuous bias tape, which is basically a long strip of fabric cut on the bias, so it allows the fabric to withstand a lot of use.

WORKING WITH FABRIC

Prewashing and Why You Really, Really Should

When a fresh bolt of brand-new fabric comes into my house, so perfect and folded and smooth, I want to cut into it so desperately that my hands actually itch. The sorry news is that all fabrics shrink when laundered or dry-cleaned, and often that shrinkage can ruin what was a perfectly stitched project. Imagine laboring over a flawless blouse only to find after it's washed that you can't quite get the buttons done. Or having your new favorite wool skirt come back from the dry cleaners small enough to fit your kid sister. Miserable.

The rule is: Treat your fabric before you cut it in the same way you'll treat the garment after it's finished. So, if you're working on re-covering your sofa with stain-resistant fabric that you'll never, ever wash? No need to prewash the fabric—hooray! But if you're working with a quilt-weight cotton on a cute little A-line skirt for the summer, you'd best wash and dry it first. If you're working with a fabric that you'll dry-clean later, like a soft supple wool for a winter wrap, send the yardage to the dry cleaner in advance and have it cleaned. (If your cleaner won't do yardage, do yourself a favor: Get a new cleaner—if he won't do flat fabric, he's probably not doing such a hot job on your heavily pleated silk dress, either.)

Check out this handy demonstration: On the right, a 4" × 4" (10cm × 10cm) swatch of quilt-weight cotton, unwashed. On the left, the same swatch after laundering. Shocking, isn't it?

Ironing and Why It Doesn't Suck That Much

When I was a kid, my mom would pay me twenty-five cents a piece to do the ironing. Although I'm sure this was intended to encourage me to earn my own spending money, all it really did was create a penniless girl who wore wrinkled clothes. The good news is, if you feel like I do, you don't have to hate ironing anymore!

When you use the iron to press your sewing, it's less about appearance and more about function. You need to press down seams and curves to help the fabric lie properly so that in the next step, you'll be able to get the project closer to the goal shape. The good news is that pressing doesn't imply hours of drudgery.

IRONING VERSUS PRESSING—USING GOOD TECHNIQUE

Most of us don't think about the nuances of ironing very much. In reality, ironing and pressing are very different things, and they're used under different circumstances. Ironing involves a back-and-forth motion that is intended to smooth out wrinkles from fabric. Good ironing uses the proper heat setting and a firm but gentle touch to return the garment or fabric to its prewashed, wrinkle-free state. Most of the ironing you'll do in a sewing project is actually pressing. Pressing involves an up-and-down motion that is intended to flatten and shape fabric as a project is being stitched. Good pressing occurs between steps during sewing and allows you to reduce the bulk of seams, shape a curve or put in a hem. Remember that both gravity and elbow grease are your friends, and don't be afraid to use pressure. Avoid hanging out with the iron on the fabric in one place for too long, though, because your project is likely to scorch.

Cutting and Keeping It Straight

As I mentioned before, cutting is a crucial step—not to put any pressure on you or anything. Because you often use the edge of your fabric to run along the seam guides, if they're uneven your seams will also be. Getting straight cuts with shears is easier than you might think. All you need is a proper cutting technique.

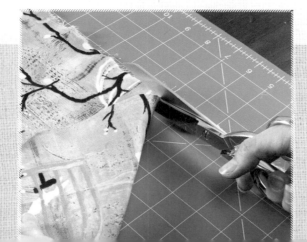

PROPER CUTTING TECHNIQUE
Keep the lower blade parallel to and in contact with the cutting surface to give you some traction and help keep a straight line. Keep very steady against the work surface and move just the upper blade.

Mini-Project CONTINUOUS BIAS TAPE

shopping list + supplies

Basic Sewing Supplies (see page 23)

18" × 22" (46cm × 56cm) piece of fabric (quilt-weight cotton or any other fabric of your choice) called a fat quarter

matching thread

marking chalk (or other marking tool)

clear acrylic ruler

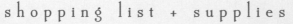

When a fabric is folded along the warp or weft, you've essentially exposed a single thread to wear and tear. When the same fabric is folded along the bias, it allows the fabric to withstand much more use and gives it a longer lifespan. I sew a lot, and a good proportion of my projects are for my home; after putting in all that time and thought and effort, and choosing fabric I really love, I want those projects to be around a while. This is especially true of things like blankets, place mats, napkins and towels, which not only take a real beating but also often see the inside of the washing machine.

For this reason, I like to use bias tape for edging a lot of my projects. Bias tape, very simply, is just a strip of fabric cut on the bias—that 45-degree angle running diagonally across the grainline of the fabric. It has the most give you can get out of a particular cut of fabric, and it allows you to bind curves and seams, wrap piping, or edge finish a project. Because it exposes many, many threads along the outer edge, bias tape has more wear capability. It's great stuff—I use it all the time, and knowing how to make and apply it will revolutionize your sewing. There is store-bought bias tape, but it's never in the colors I work with, and never the length I need; I prefer the creative freedom that comes from making my own.

You can easily make small bias strips just by slicing across that bias line. This is the technique I use when binding armholes, necklines and other relatively short items. When I need a longer piece, though, I'd be forced to stitch each of those strips together into one longer strip, and that's a huge pain in the behind as far as I'm concerned. It's much easier to make continuous bias tape (CBT) by stitching a larger piece of fabric together on the bias and then cutting that into a long strip. You get piles and piles of bias tape this way, and you get the freedom to choose any fabric you want, rather than being limited to the solid, poly-cotton blend available at the fabric stores. You can also manipulate the width of the bias tape better.

So how do you make CBT? Turn the page to find out! As you're stitching remember this: the first time can be a rough road, especially if you're teaching yourself, so give yourself some slack. But after that it's such a quick, simple process that I know you'll make it a regular part of your sewing time.

Cuts of Fabric

Many versions of CBT instructions have you begin with a square of fabric. Because a cut of fabric is a rectangle, it makes more sense to me to begin with a rectangle than a square, and it's also a more economical use of your fabric. So that's what you'll use here.

As you can see in the supplies list, you'll use a fat quarter of fabric to make the bias tape. In the future, you can use any length of fabric. How much depends on how long you want your finished bias tape to be. But the smaller the piece, the easier it is to manipulate without getting overwhelmed.

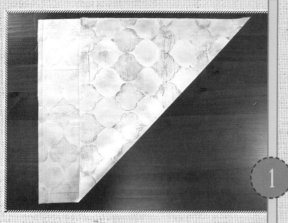

1. FOLD FABRIC

Cut off the selvages of your fabric. (Remember, selvage edges shrink at a different rate than the remainder of your fabric and should always be removed, even if it feels like a huge waste of a straight edge).

Place the fabric so the longer edges are on the top and bottom. Fold the bottom right corner up so the bottom edge meets the top edge, forming a triangle with a little left over.

2. CUT ALONG DIAGONAL

Cut the fabric along the triangle's fold (the diagonal). You should end up with two pieces of fabric: one a triangle and one an odd, nameless geometric shape with four sides that looks almost like a triangle.

3. STACK PIECES, MATCHING EDGES

Flip both pieces of fabric over so the odd shape is facing up and the triangle is facing down. Place the triangle on top of the odd shape, lining up the edges. You should now have an odd, four-sided shape that looks kind of like a mouth.

4. STITCH PIECES TOGETHER

Take the fabric to the machine and stitch the pieces together along the edge using a ¼" (6mm) seam allowance. (See pages 49–50 for a reminder about seam allowances and basic stitching.) Remember to backtack at both ends and trim the threads close to the project. You'll know you got it right if, when you open up the fabric, the shape is a parallelogram.

5. PRESS OPEN SEAM ALLOWANCS

Nearly every time you stitch two pieces of fabric together, you'll need to press your seam allowances. Sometimes you'll press them open and sometimes in a particular direction. Here, press the seam allowances open like a butterfly by using the weight and heat of the iron to press the fabric edges away from one another to reveal the seam line in the center.

6. DRAW LINES ON BIAS

Keep the fabric face down (with the seam allowances facing up at you). Starting at one angled edge, begin drawing lines parallel to the bias angle (the diagonal edge) and marching across the fabric. (I use quilting chalk for this, but whatever marking tool you prefer is fine.) Usually, how far apart you space the lines depends on how fat you want your bias strip to be. For this example use a width of 3" (8cm). I space my lines with a quilting ruler since it's clear and acrylic and sticky on the bottom, making my marks more consistent—and consistency is the key with this step. The widths don't have to be absolutely perfect, but the closer they are the easier the next steps will be.

7. TRIM OFF VESTIGE

At the end of the fabric, you may not have a full width left. Cut that paltry little vestige off to make sure each of your strips is of equal size.

Stitch Tip

Check out the CBT guide on the book CD. It includes guides that you can print out to help you as you draw the lines. The guide offers you three different widths; I'd like to respectfully suggest starting with the largest of them.

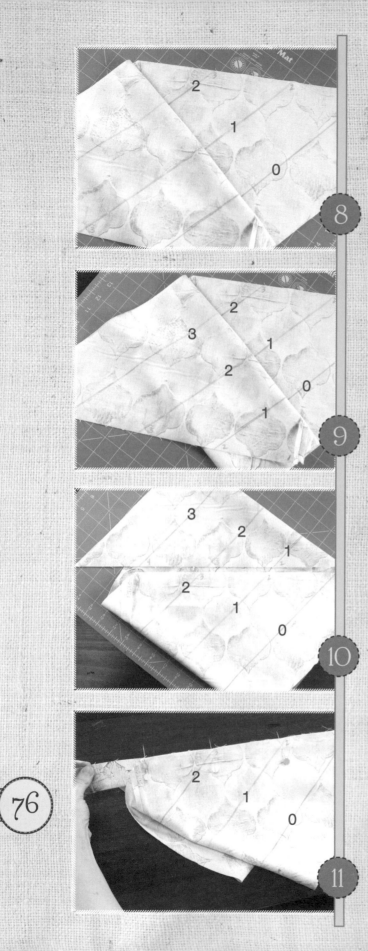

8. NUMBER LINES ON ONE EDGE

Here comes the confusing part, at least for most people. The goal is to create a tube of fabric (steps 11 and 12) and then cut that tube apart (step 13) to make a long strip. Now, you don't want to stitch a tube and then cut it apart into a series of donuts, so the edge you stitch needs to be slightly offset. To achieve this, number the lines you just drew. Start at the straight (not bias) edge on one side with number 0 and move up to each line sequentially (the next line is 1, the next is 2, etc).

9. NUMBER LINES ON OTHER EDGE

Repeat step 8 on the opposite straight edge, but this time, begin with 1 instead of 0.

10: MATCH LINES AND NUMBERS

Turn the fabric over so the print is facing up (and the chalk lines are facing the cutting surface). Bring the two straight edges (i.e., the edges with the numbers, not the bias edges) together so the numbered lines match: line 1 meets line 1, line 2 meets line 2, etc.

11. PIN EDGES

Line up the numbers with the edges together and pin in place. This step feels a little awkward because it makes a twisted tube of fabric, but that's how it's supposed to end up—offset.

Bear in mind that as you match these lines up, the corners do not match, the lines along one raw edge are heading off to the left, and the lines along the other raw edge are heading off to the right. While it looks as though we want them to meet one another at the raw edge, in order for them to become one continuous line, we really want them to meet where the seam line will be. So instead of making the lines match where the two pieces of fabric come together (along the edge), shift the edge of the fabric facing you to the left so that the lines heading off to your left cross the lines on the rear fabric at the seam line— hold the fabric up to the light and you'll see this more clearly. If you put a pin through the line on one side of the fabric your seam allowance distance from the edge (i.e., ½" [1.3cm]), it should be going through the line on the other side of the fabric, as well. If not, keep shifting until that happens. Also, if you have a choice between having the lines match perfectly and the fabric lying flat, just keep pinning and matching the best you can—it's much more important that your seam lies flat than that your numbers and lines match flawlessly.

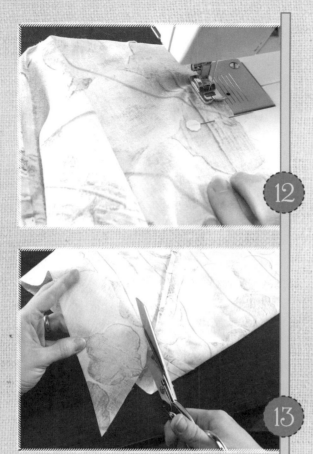

12. STITCH SEAM

Take your twisted tube to the machine and stitch a seam along the edge you just pinned, using a ¼" (6mm) seam allowance. Keep reaching beneath your work as you sew to make sure there are no catches or random bits of fabric getting caught under the needle. Then press that awkward seam open. (A sleeve board is great for this, but your ironing board will work, too.)

13. CUT ALONG CHALK LINE

This is where the magic happens. At each end of your tube, you have a little tail of fabric hanging off (the unmatched corners). You also now have a single line of chalk going around and around the fabric. Choose one end of the tube—it doesn't matter which one—and begin cutting the first marked line next to that little tail. I usually put the fabric on my arm like a sleeve to be sure I cut through only one layer at this step.

14. FINISH CUTTING

Keep cutting along the marked line all the way around, through a single layer of fabric, and watch as the tape begins to take form. When you come to one of your seams that you've pressed open, cut right across it and keep going.

Ta-da! The finished product: yards and yards of bias tape from your favorite fabric. I make lots of this at once when I have the time and then store it for different projects. That way, I get the enjoyment of it, and I use my time economically.

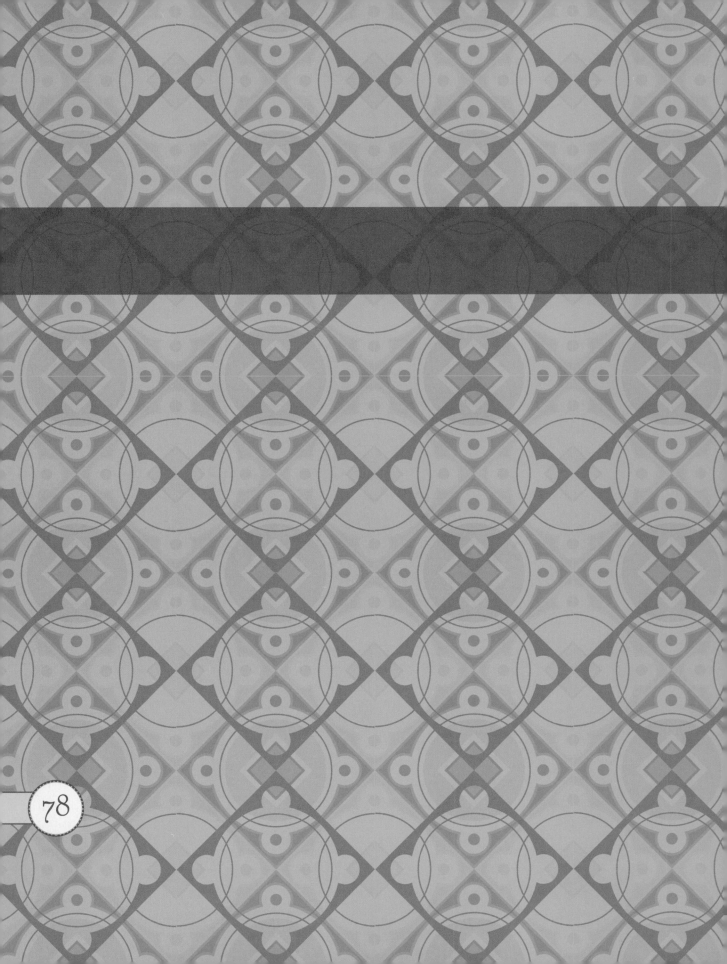

PART TWO:
THE LESSONS

FOUNDATIONAL SKILLS: HOME DECOR AND PERSONAL STYLE PROJECTS

Each of the projects that follow is super cute, yes, but each of them is also carefully designed to cover basic skills while you work. Plenty of "learn to sew" books either give you next-to-no information on actually learning to sew and instead focus on a whole mess of projects, or they teach you to sew by making one project, and at the end of the day, all you know how to make is that one thing—like pajama pants or a Halloween door hanger. And let's be honest, how many Halloween door hangers do you really need? Worse still, some are encyclopedic in their approach and are totally intimidating. How can you learn to sew if you're confronted with a zillion skills and no one tells you when and where to use them?

Instead, these projects have been designed so you get the instant gratification of creating each project, but as you work, you also soak up all the essential skills necessary to create anything else you have in mind. I always assume that you want to learn to sew because you already have ideas, and you're looking to find the mechanical skills to bring those ideas to life. That's what we'll do here, and as we go along, I'll give suggestions for how to extrapolate these skills and apply them to other projects. Ready?

FANCY NAPKIN
WITH MITERED CORNERS

Let's start with a project that will reinforce all that good stitching technique you've been practicing, and teach you how to make the neatest, tidiest corners you ever saw: a simple cloth napkin. At our house, I've broken my husband of the paper towel habit, and we use cloth napkins for everything. The ones you'll make here are very simple and suitable for breakfast or picnics. After you finish those, you can try some of the corner variations that will take these all the way up to Suitable for Company. I love that this project gives instant gratification while also allowing you to work at your level. This is also a fantastic chance to practice your straight stitching and get to be a total pro before moving on to some more complicated projects.

shopping list + supplies

Basic Sewing Tools (see page 23)

1¼ yards (1.1m) of quilt-weight cotton fabric (for four napkins)

matching thread

rotary cutter, cutting mat and acrylic ruler (optional)

marking chalk

• • •

skills you'll build

stitching straight lines

mitering corners

pivoting

edge finishing with a zigzag stitch

83

Finding the Grainline

Locating the grainline on your fabric ensures that the shape you're stitching will remain after laundering and allows you to cut the straightest line possible. Now, most fabric is cut by friendly humans so the edges are rarely perfect. To find the grainline of the fabric, you need to true up the edges (square them up). There are two techniques for doing this: pulling and ripping. They both sound like fun, don't they?

OPTION A: PULLING

Pulling a single thread from the warp of the fabric automatically reveals the fabric's natural grainline. It's a little time-consuming, but for delicate and expensive fabrics, it really is the better option because it's gentler on the fabric. This technique can be used in either direction to create a clean, smooth corner on your fabric.

1. TEASE OUT THREAD

Find the selvage of your fabric and then tease out one or two threads using a pin.

2. PULL ALONG LENGTH OF THREAD

Continue to pull the thread along its length until you've revealed a line. You can mark the line with chalk, if you'd like.

OPTION B: RIPPING

Ripping, on the other hand, while not as gentle, is fast and effective. When fabric is torn across the weft, it tears along a single thread line, accurately revealing the grainline.

1. SNIP AND RIP

To rip, snip the fabric first. Then rip away! This technique may leave you with slightly curling edges, which can be smoothed out with the iron. After using this method to find the crossgrain, your fabric might still be slighty skewed. Grab two corners diagonal to one another and give a firm pull. The fabric should pop back square.

Cutting a Square

Now that you've established the grainline of your fabric, you're going to cut a 19" (48cm) square. At this point, you might wonder why we even bothered with that last step at all: Won't the crookedness of any bad cutting at the fabric shop just fall away? Well, yes and no. Yes, if the fabric was cut unevenly to start with, you can remove those edges and make a new, straight cut. If your new cut, though, isn't along the grainline, as you use and launder your napkins, they tend to shift and bunch and become unsquared as those threads pull against one another and fight to return to their natural, squared state. You're really better off truing up the fabric at the start—it's time well invested.

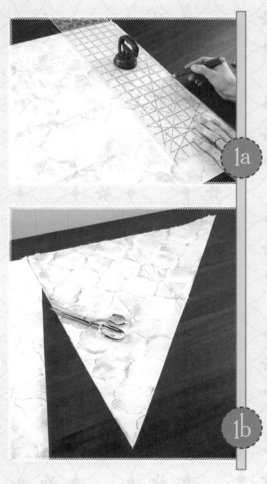

So, for that square. There are two ways to do it.

OPTION A: TRADITIONAL METHOD

I've had plenty of students who prefer to do things this way, and are bothered if they don't.

1. MEASURE AND CUT

Measure out all four sides using an acrylic ruler and mark the lines with chalk. Then cut out each side.

OPTION B: THE CHEATER METHOD

I have other students who feel overwhelmed by the idea of getting the four sides of their square to line up just right and measure out properly. They prefer to use their high school geometry.

1. MEASURE TWO SIDES AND FOLD

Measure out one side of the square along the edge you've trued up. Then measure another perpendicular to the first. Fold the first line up to lie along the second, and you've made a square. Cut off the excess, and the folded-over triangle opens out to becomes a square just the right measurements!

Believe it or not, you're almost halfway to having your napkin complete!

Completing the Overcast Edge Finish

If you check out the inside of probably any garment you're wearing, you'll notice that the seam allowances have been wrapped in multiple threads. This is done with the help of a specialized machine called a serger. For most folks new to sewing, investing in another machine when you're not even sure you're in love with your sewing machine yet can be a daunting prospect. Luckily, you have other options when it comes to finishing the edges of projects.

You're going to use the zigzag stitch on your sewing machine to mimic the effects of the serger and prevent your project from getting all raggedy in the washer. This technique—creating overcase edges—can be used on many projects (see the sidebar on the next page), and makes a finished product not only look better, but last longer, too.

What's a Serger?

Sergers (also—and more correctly—called overlock machines) are similar to sewing machines in that they have upper and lower threads, but they have three or four of them instead of two, and include a cutting blade that allows them to stitch, trim and finish the seam all in one step. They're used in addition to a sewing machine (rather than in place of it) and are usually considered advanced equipment.

1

1. ZIGZAG STITCH DOWN ONE EDGE

Set your sewing machine to the widest zigzag stitch you have available and your default stitch length. This gives you plenty of wiggle room as you determine the look you prefer for this technique.

Start stitching in the middle of a side (the corners tend to get driven down into the hole in your throat plate). Place your fabric beneath your needle, lining up your fabric so the cut edge runs directly beneath the needle; you'll be sending the cut edge right down the center of the presser foot.

2. STITCH EDGE

Now, stitch down the edge, making your way to a corner. You'll see that the zigzag stitch places the needle so that with each stitch it goes on the fabric, off the fabric, on the fabric, off the fabric. As that happens, the thread pulls up around the outer cut edge of your fabric, wrapping it (and perhaps slightly rolling it) and preventing it from unraveling.

3. PIVOT AROUND CORNER

When you reach the corner, stop with your needle in the fabric, lift your presser foot and rotate the fabric on the needle to turn the corner. Lower your presser foot and begin stitching again along the next edge. Continue stitching and pivoting until all edges are stitched.

Overcasting: Super Useful!

Where else would you use an overcast edge? How about, where wouldn't you use one? It's a great technique for finishing the edge of any project where you know the edges won't be folded under or stitched over. How about when you sew a garment? Overcast the edges of all of the cut pieces before stitching them together, and prevent unraveling before it starts! You can also use a simple overcast edge anywhere you don't need to be concerned about hemming or finishing a project: curtains for your kids' puppet theater or goody bags made from fabric.

Mitering the Corners

That edge finish is really all you need to make a completed napkin. In fact, my mother made a set of napkins this way back in 1976 that I used the last time I visited her, and they're still fantastic. Having said that, this is a pretty casual kind of napkin, the kind that's suitable for picnics or breakfast with the family. They're not, maybe, quite what you'd like to offer dinner guests (or your mother-in-law; am I right?). For that, we'll do another step: mitering the corners.

Think of the wood trim along your bedroom door. It's not two tall pieces topped by a third piece cut square, like the monuments at Stonehenge. Instead, each piece has been cut at a 45-degree angle so the corners meet cleanly and attractively. This is the same principle you'll be using here: You want the corners to be folded in and the edges folded back, and you want to ensure that none of the unfinished edges are exposed. Mitering corners not only makes for a prettier finished project, but it also eliminates bulk.

1. FOLD BACK CORNERS AND PRESS

First, head to your ironing board. Place the napkin right side down. Fold back each corner about ¾" (2cm) and press in place.

2. FOLD EDGE OF NAPKIN

Fold over one side of the napkin, making the edge of that side meet up with the point on the corner you've folded back. Press the edge in place.

3. FOLD OTHER EDGES TO MAKE MITERED CORNERS

Repeat on the other three sides until all four corners share the same tidy 45-degree angle.

Topstitching

Any time you create stitches that run parallel to a fold or stitch line, you're topstitching. For your napkin, you can choose to topstitch either with your straight stitch or with your zigzag. Either way, your stitches will be visible from the right side of your project, a point you're wise to keep in mind as you work. Hey, why not even consider using a contrasting thread? Or maybe your machine makes specialty stitches, like flowers or tiny dogs. As long as you're going to be able to see the stitches, you might as well make them pop.

TOPSTITCH ALONG EDGE

Starting along one straight edge, stitch close to the zigzag stitches along each side. Pivot when you reach the corners and continue around the perimeter of your napkin until you arrive back where you began.

Remember, you're not stitching close to the fold: This would allow the zigzagged edge to fold back over itself unattractively, and you don't want that. Instead, aim to keep your stitches directly over your finished edge. The secret to good topstitching is to maintain your consistency—after that, there's nothing to it!

Guess what? You've completed the project! Now just repeat the steps to complete the other three napkins. And turn the pages for some fancier options and inspiration.

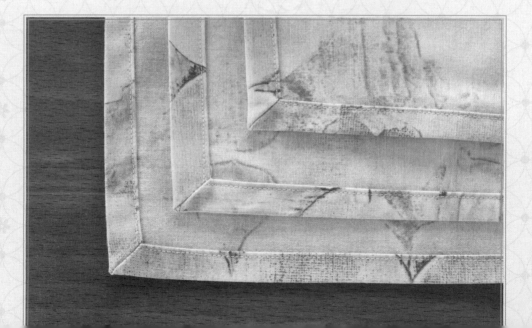

Varsity Mitered Corner

For a truly professional finish you can stitch your miters first. Go, take a look at those fancy cloth napkins in the big box housewares stores: Theirs are totally done the same way. Here's a mini-lesson in how to do just that.

1. FOLD EDGES UNDER TWICE

Place the napkin right side down. Fold up one edge ¼" (6mm). Press the fold in place. Fold up a second time, another ¼" (6mm). Press the edges in place again. Repeat on the three remaining sides. Make sure you get a crisp fold line from your pressing; you'll need to see the lines in the next step.

2. DRAW CHALK LINE AT CORNER

Open your folded edges so the napkin is flat. Draw a line at a diagonal across the corner, at the tip of where the pressed lines (shown by the dotted lines in the photo) intersect. Repeat with the other three corners.

3. FOLD NAPKIN AND STITCH CORNER

Fold all four edges in along the first pressed fold line (¼" [6mm]). Fold the napkin right sides together along a diagonal, so the corner comes to a point, matching the diagonal chalk line front and back. Stitch along the chalk line—your stitches should go through the chalk line on both front and back of the point. Repeat on the other three corners.

4. TRIM CORNER

Trim your corner to within ¼" (6mm) of the stitched (chalk) line. (Do not snip through your stitches!) Repeat with the other three corners.

5. TURN CORNER RIGHT SIDE OUT

Pop the corner so it's right side out and press it. Repeat with the other three corners. Turn all four edges in along the second pressed fold line (¼" [6mm]).

6. PRESS AND TOPSTITCH

Press all the way around your napkin so everything is nice and neat. Then topstitch very close to the inside folded edge. Gorgeous and so professional!

Edge Finish Options

Full Miter

With the full miter, the edge finish becomes unnecessary because turning under the raw edge of the fabric and tucking it away prevents any fraying. This makes a nice, formal edge.

Half-Miter

The half-miter takes advantage of either the overcast or the serged edge finish, but adds a folded hem with a fancy corner.

Serged Edge

A serged edge can be a standard serged finish or a fancy rolled hem, and it creates a casual edge.

Overcast Edge

A simple overcast finish can be done on any sewing machine and is a long-lasting method to prevent edges from fraying. For fabrics that are resistant to the overcast edge, try stitching inside the edge of your fabric and trim super close—but not through!—the stitches.

FOR MORE INSPIRATION

When making your napkins, the stitches holding your folded sides in place don't have to be straight! Here's a great chance for you to play with color and stitch variation. How about a napkin with contrasting thread? Or one with your specialty stitches along the fold line? Your guests will be paying attention only to the front of the napkin, so they'll see the square of fancy stitches following the edge of the fabric and think you're the coolest, craftiest kid in town.

PICNIC PLACE MAT
WITH BIAS-BOUND EDGES

XXXXXXXXXXXXXXXXXXXXXXXXXXXXXXXXXXXXXXXXXXXXXXXXXXXXXXXXX

Now that you've made a fancy napkin suitable for any event,
let's put together the perfect place mat to go with it: one that
travels wherever you do! This project is very adaptable, so
while you're making a place mat, you'll be learning skills to
bind the edges of almost anything, create pockets almost
anywhere and complete multiple steps with one stitch.

shopping list + supplies

Basic Sewing Tools
(see page 23)

½ yard (26cm) of fabric
for body of place mat

2¼ yards (2.1m) of
continuous bias tape 3"
(8cm) wide in contrasting
fabric for binding

¾ yard (69cm) of ribbon

matching thread

skills you'll build

identifying right side
versus wrong side

applying bias tape

binding edges

inserting ribbon

stitching the ditch

channel stitching

combining fabrics

95

What's a Fat Quarter?

In this project, you'll be working with a size of fabric called a fat quarter. If you don't come to sewing as a quilter, you may not be familiar with this term. This cut of fabric has been marketed mostly to quilters as a great way to get more prints and colors without needing to invest in whole yards. I think of it as a great craft cut, though, one that allows you to test out a lot of different projects with a minimal investment of money and space.

If a full yard of a 45" (1.1m) fabric measures 36" × 45" (91cm × 114cm) and a half yard measures 18" × 45" (46cm × 114cm) , then a quarter yard measures 9" × 45" (23cm × 114cm). The problem is that a quarter yard (in these dimensions, called a "skinny quarter") isn't a very versatile dimension. Instead, fat quarters are half of a half yard, or 18" × 22" (46cm × 56cm), and give you a more square-ish area to work with.

fat quarter

quarter yard (skinny quarter)

FAT QUARTER SEWING PROJECTS

We're using fat quarters for a number of projects in the book, but a quick check on the Web will reveal hundreds of fat quarter projects just dying to be made! All the items here—flip flops, pin cushion and notebook cover—were made with a single fat quarter of fabric.

Working with Right Sides and Wrong Sides

I already talked about prints on fabrics having a top and bottom, a direction. Fabric that's been printed also has a right side and a wrong side: On the right side, the inks have been printed, and on the wrong side, we see the reflection of that. We don't call these the top and bottom or front and back of the fabric because your project also has a top and bottom and a front and back, and using all those terms together can get pretty confusing.

On a printed fabric, it's pretty obvious which side is the right side and which is the wrong side. The same thing is true of corduroys and velvets, where there's a pile on one side and none on the other. With twills, it's a little tougher: If you peer closely, you'll see a slight diagonal texture created by the weave of the fabric; that's your right side. On some fabrics, like solid cottons, it's nearly impossible to tell which is the right side and which is the wrong side. The answer in those cases is if you can't tell, no one else can, either. Just choose one to be the right side and be consistent with it throughout your project. For one thing, there might be slight variations that aren't apparent at the beginning but could show up in another light, and for another, many pattern pieces are cut out as mirror images, and it's best to know which is which to avoid mixing up left and right. One way to do that is to mark each pattern piece as you cut it out on the right side using chalk or disappearing pen; then you'll always know which side is the right side.

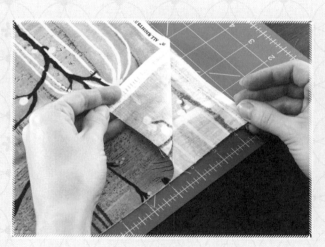

Wrong sides together

In the projects, I'll often refer to putting the right sides or wrong sides together. This photo shows a printed cotton fabric with the wrong sides together and the right sides on the outside.

When working on a project, you should always be aware of the right side and wrong side of the fabric. In some circumstances, it's necessary to take two pieces of fabric that each have a right side and a wrong side and create a single piece of fabric that has two right sides. Later on in this project, for example, you'll fold up the bottom edge of your place mat in order to form the pocket. When you do that, you'll expose the underside of the fabric; if it's a single thickness, that means the wrong side of your fabric would be showing, and that's not the pretty, professional product we're going for. Instead, you're going to make a single piece of fabric that has two right sides out of two pieces of fabric that have one right side and one wrong side.

Cutting the Squares

While working on your napkins, you created a straight line by truing up your grainline and following that edge for a straight cut. But what about when that's not practical, or when you need a longer line? Or how about when you true up your grainline and still struggle to cut a clean, straight line? There really is an art to cutting well, and it's a huge part of sewing. Fortunately, it's also a skill that can be learned.

For this place mat, you'll need to cut two pieces of fabric approximately 18" (46cm) square. (They don't have to be exactly 18" [46cm]—that's just the dimension that your eye will tell you is "right" for a place mat.) You're starting with a ½ yard (46cm), which is already 18" (46cm) along one side, making measuring easy.

1. FOLD FABRIC IN HALF

With the wrong sides together, fold the fabric in half.

Why? The easiest way to cut the squares out is through a double thickness of fabric. It's always best to make pieces that will be stitched to one another as symmetrical as possible, and cutting them out at the same time will certainly do that. By cutting through two layers of fabric at the same time, not only do you prevent slipping and sliding (because the weight and slight static between the two layers hold the fabric in place better), but you'll also guarantee that if the pieces are asymmetrical, they're equally asymmetrical.

2. CUT SQUARES

Cut out your square (using one of the methods on page 85). Remember, to get straight lines, your goal is to keep the lower blade very steady against the work surface and move just the upper blade. If you're using a rotary blade rather than shears, take your time, and really watch those curves.

Basting

As you know, your sewing machine allows you to adjust the length of your stitches, from zero (no length) to its top level (probably four or six, which is a very long stitch). This longest stitch is your basting stitch. Basting is temporary stitching that is used to hold fabric in place prior to putting in the final stitches. Pins are usually used to hold fabric in place, but sometimes pins just won't do the trick: when you're putting together a dress, for example, and want to try it on to check the fit, or when too many pins would simply get in the way, as in this case.

Basting stitches should be put along the stitch line for your project to ensure that you're holding the fabric together in the place where it will be stitched in the final steps. Basting stitches are then removed after the real stitches are put in, so they don't sully the prettiness of what you've created. Now, I don't know about you but that sounds like twice the work to me, and is the reason why I have steadfastly avoided basting on most projects for most of my life. (When I began to stitch more investment pieces, though, I began to see the value of basting: If I'm making a gorgeous fitted jacket out of super-nice and expensive fabric, I really want to be sure I get it right the first time. Believe it or not, basting lets you do that by test-driving the fit before you commit to the final, hard-to-remove stitches.)

For this project, we're going to throw that whole baste-on-the-stitch-line rule out the window. We'll baste *inside* the stitch line. That way, you won't be required to remove the stitches later. Because fit is not an issue here, you can afford to cut a little corner and make your work both easier and beautiful.

BASTE EDGES

Place the two squares of fabric wrong sides together.

Before you start stitching, think about the direction of your print. Because you'll be folding up the lower edge to create the pocket, if both pieces of fabric are one-way direction fabrics, and both are pointing the same way, then the print on the pocket will be upside down. To avoid this, take the lower piece of fabric and rotate it 180 degrees so it's upside down in relation to the front piece. That way, when you fold up your pocket, all the images will be pointed in the same direction!

At the machine, baste the two squares around all four sides using a ⅜" (1cm) seam allowance. Pivot at the corners, but don't backtack.

Binding the Pocket

Now that you have the body of the place mat complete, let's begin the binding process using your continuous bias tape. First, the edge of the pocket gets bound.

1. PRESS EDGES OF BIAS TAPE

Cut a 60" (1.5m) long piece of bias tape 3" (8cm) wide (long enough to go around three sides of the place mat plus 6" [15cm]). Cut a second piece of bias tape 20" (51cm) long (the length of one edge). Then turn the raw edges of the bias tape to the inside on both long edges about ⅝" (1.6cm). Press the folds in place. I like to use my bias tape maker (shown here) to keep my fingers from getting scorched, but you can press without one as well.

2. PIN BIAS TAPE TO EDGE OF PLACE MAT

Turn your place mat right side up so the least perfect long edge is at the bottom. (If all of your sides are perfect, good for you! Just make an executive decision.) Fold that edge up until it lies in the center of the mat—sort of like folding a letter to put in an envelope, but you're only folding one edge up. (This will create the pocket later on when we stitch it in place; for now, folding it up just helps you see where the bias tape goes.)

Open one fold of the 20" (51cm) bias tape. Lay the tape with that raw edge along the raw edge of the pocket, right sides together. Pin the bias tape in place, being careful to pin just the pocket and not the back of the place mat, too. Place the pins perpendicular to the edge.

3. STITCH BIAS TAPE IN PLACE

Now that the bias tape fold is opened up, you have a nice, clean fold to use as a stitch guide. Unfold the pocket so the two squares lie flat with the bias tape pinned along one edge. Using the fold line as a guide, stitch the bias tape in place. Stitch all the way down the length of that one side, using the fold line as the stitch guide. (For the record, if your pins are placed perpendicular to the stitch line, it's safe to stitch over them.)

If the cut edges of your bias tape are slightly uneven, check to be sure that the folded edge is straight as it relates to the edge of the place mat. No one will ever see the inner edge of the bias tape (because you'll be stitching it down), but they're sure going to notice if your binding is at a 30-degree angle.

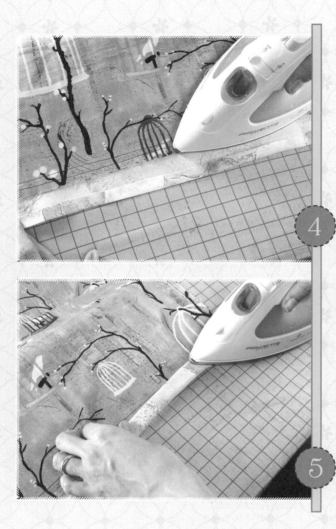

4. PRESS SEAM ALLOWANCES TOWARD BIAS TAPE

You'll recall from the continuous bias tape project (on pages 72–77) that you usually need to press the seam allowance after stitching pieces together. In this case, press your seam allowances toward your bias tape.

This is a popular instruction in commercial patterns: telling you to press your seam allowances in a particular direction. It just means that rather than pressing the two seam allowances apart and away from one another, you treat them as one and press them in a particular direction. For this project, it permits you to later fold them inside the bias tape and mask them from view.

5. FOLD BIAS TAPE AND PIN

Take the pressed edge of the bias tape—the one that's folded under—and double it over so the folded edge is on the back of the place mat, enclosing the raw edges of the seam allowance like a clam shell. Extend the tape edge just beyond the stitch line on the place mat. (You will be covering the stitches of the seam you sewed in step 2, but only barely.)

Now, here's a little confession: In most situations, I really don't pin that much when I stitch. For long, straight seams where I can see both raw edges that I'll be joining, I don't want to risk introducing inaccuracies or spend the time correcting mistakes. However, when stitching the ditch (which you'll learn on the next page), I definitely pin: I can't see the edge I'm stitching down, and I want to be sure I catch it.

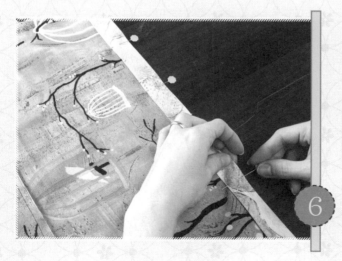

6. PIN BIAS TAPE IN PLACE

Once the bias tape is folded over the raw edge, pin the bias tape edge to the place mat.

Stitching the Ditch

Stitching the ditch, or gutter stitching, is a technique that allows you to make your stitches nearly invisible. You accomplish this by placing a new set of stitches directly on top of a previous set, hiding them in the ditch where two fabrics join (hence the term). This is a common technique to use on waistbands that makes them ever-so-slightly more formal.

1. TEASE APART SEAM

Flip the place mat over to the front so you can see the seam you just stitched (in step 3 on page 100). If you place slight horizontal pressure on the place mat and bias tape, you can clearly see the thread. This is where you'll aim your needle when you stitch the ditch. If it lands directly on top of the previous stitches and then you release the pressure, the fabric will fold back toward the seam line and disguise those stitches, making them all but invisible.

2. STITCH THE DITCH

Place the place mat on the machine with the pin side down. Place the seam line directly under the needle. Stitch down that line, removing your pins just before you get to them. Your goal here is to get that needle directly on top of those previous stitches so they'll be hidden after you're done.

With all of your invisible stitches in place, head back to the iron and press that newly bound edge to make it nice and crisp.

As I mentioned earlier, it's totally safe to stitch over pins—except in the case of stitching the ditch. When you place the pin perpendicular to the stitch line, it distorts the shape ever so slightly. This might not make a difference in a simple seam, but for stitching the ditch, it pulls stitches away from a straight line and prevents them from being invisible.

3. FOLD UP BOTTOM EDGE TO FORM POCKET

You'll recall in step 2 on page 100 that you folded up the edge for the pocket. Now that you've bound the pocket edge, here's where you'll really set the pocket in place.

Fold up the bound edge of the place mat with the visible stitches to the inside. Place the bound edge where you had it previously: about halfway up the place mat so you create a pocket with the fold at the lower place mat edge.

Binding the Place Mat Edges

This next section is somewhat longer than the previous ones, but after you complete it, you'll be nearly done! You're binding three edges of the place mat (not all four, and I'll tell you why in a minute). As you do that, you'll also catch the pocket and stitch it in place and secure a ribbon to tie the whole thing shut. Many birds, one stone! For the binding, you'll use a quilt-binding technique that gives sharp, clean corners and is a fantastic skill to have in your back pocket.

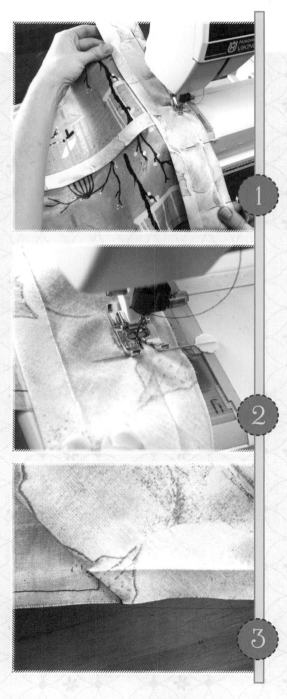

1. PIN BIAS TAPE ALONG SHORT EDGE

Start by setting the place mat with the folded edge of the pocket to your north (which is actually the bottom) and the raw edge at the bottom. Lay out the 60" (1.5m) bias tape along the right edge (your east). At this folded edge, leave about 2" (5cm) hanging off the edge; the entire length of tape will hang off the raw bottom edge. Place the bias tape right side down on top of the place mat and make sure the raw edges line up. Pin the tape in place.

Set the place mat on the machine with the folded pocket edge at the top and the raw edge at the bottom.

2. STOP AT SEAM ALLOWANCE

Place a pin at the seam allowance (which is the same measurement as the width of the fold along the edge of your bias tape) along the bottom edge. Stitch the bias tape in place along the fold line just like you did on the pocket edge (step 3 on page 100). Stitch until you reach the pin and then backtack. (You have to do this in order to create the fancy fold finish that gives you the pretty corners you want.) When you're finished, place the project on your work surface with the folded pocket edge at the top.

3. FOLD END OF BIAS TAPE OUT

Fold the tail end of the bias tape away from the edge you're preparing to bind (the top edge of the place mat). As you fold, you should create a 45-degree angle, and the edge of the place mat should line up with the folded-out edge of the bias tape. (If they don't, go back and adjust your backtack—chances are you didn't backtack far enough up.)

5. FOLD BIAS TAPE BACK OVER PLACE MAT

Now fold the bias tape back over the edge you'll bind (along the top edge of the place mat). This creates a little triangle at the corner—see it? You want the top edge of the triangle parallel with the edge you're going to bind, and the right edge of the triangle even with the edge you just bound. The better those two edges line up, the more perfect your results will be later.

6. LINE UP EDGES

When the fold is complete, the raw edge of the bias tape should line up with the raw edge of the place mat. Pin the tape in place.

7. STITCH BIAS TAPE

Stitch in the fold of the bias tape again, backtacking at the beginning. As you stitch, you'll run right over the point of the triangle underneath. Stop and backtack at the seam allowance distance ($5/8$" [1.5cm]) from the end, just as you did in step 3.

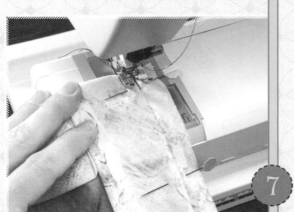

8. COMPLETE REMAINING SIDES

Repeat steps 4–6 to complete the next corner. Then complete step 7 again to stitch the third edge. This time, sew right on off the edge when you get to the end. Trim the bias tape so you have about 2" (5cm) hanging off the edge. When you're finished, turn the bias tape right side out to see your beautiful corners!

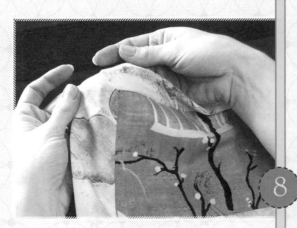

Finishing the Edges

You might have wondered why you didn't bind all four edges of the place mat. For one thing, the lower edge is already finished (because it's folded) and doesn't really need to be bound. For another, I want to demonstrate how to create a clean finish on the bottom edge of a side that's been bound. Say you have a pair of drapes that you got for your last place, but when you move to your new one, they're too narrow for the windows. Rather than toss them out, you can add panels of contrasting fabric on the right and left to widen them. To finish them off on the lower edge without adding length, you can fold the bottoms in just like you're about to do with the place mat. You'll finish these edges and then attach the rest of the binding and add the ribbon. Ready?

1. FOLD BINDING OVER FOLDED EDGE

Flip the place mat to the back, with the folded edge (the bottom) at the top. Working on the left edge first, take the 2" (5cm) tail of bias tape (see page 100) and fold it down to wrap the seam allowance. Then fold the bias tape over the edge so the corner is covered. Make sure the corner edges line up. Pin in place.

2. FOLD MITERED CORNERS

Fold the remaining bias tape all around the place mat to the back. At the corners, fold the squared edge into a triangle to mimic the mitering on the front. Pin the binding in place.

3. ATTACH RIBBON AND STITCH BINDING

Fold the piece of ribbon in half. Place the folded edge under the bias tape at the middle of one of the short edges. Pin the ribbon in place.

Stitch the ditch all the way around the place mat to secure the bias tape (and the ribbon). Pivot at the corners. Be careful to hold the ribbon away from the needle so you don't accidentally stitch it down.

Channel Stitching

Ah, the English Channel, that divisor of the mainland of Europe from the British Isles. Channel stitching is the same idea (but not as damp): rows of stitches whose purpose is to divide one section of a project from another. You'll use it here to create the pockets in your place mat.

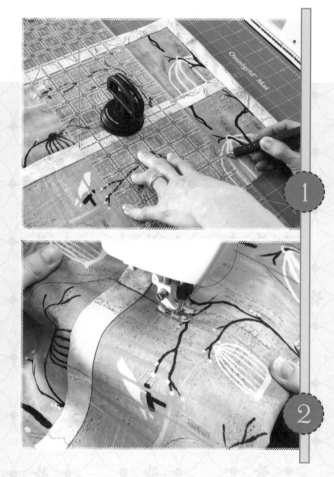

1. MARK LINES FOR POCKETS

Measure out the width you'd like your pockets to be. For this place mat—which has five pockets for napkin or menu, knife, fork, spoon and additional utensil (like chopsticks)—the first pocket is 4" (10cm) wide and the rest are 6" (15cm) wide.

Using a straight edge and your marking chalk, lightly sketch the stitch lines on top of the pocket.

2. STITCH POCKETS

Stitch each line from the top of the pocket to the bottom folded edge, backtacking at the beginning and end (be certain to stitch over the binding, otherwise it has an unattractive tendency to fold over and spoil all of your hard work!).

Sit back and admire how very, very cool your place mat is. I swear, I've seen more than a hundred of these made, and no two are ever even remotely similar—and even better, even the most suspect fabrics turn out super cute!

Stitch Tip

You can create as many pockets as you like and for whatever utensils your heart desires. Whatever you choose, keep in mind that the two-dimensional width of your pockets needs to be enough to accommodate the three-dimensional objects you'll be putting in them! Avoid making a pocket you think is for chopsticks and find out only one will fit; add additional width to each pocket.

FOR MORE INSPIRATION

Did you know you can make more than just adorable place mats with these instructions? With minor variations, you can make just about anything! Create a crayon keeper; just make a smaller, longer version of the place mat with tiny pockets. Or stitch a handy-dandy tool belt; just add ribbon to the top corners instead of the sides. Play your cards right, and there's enough fabric to make a little "hood" (shown here) to keep your toiletries cozy and safe for travel. This also makes a great knitting needle keeper.

Your newfound bias-binding knowledge will be handy for a variety of projects in addition to picnic place mats. Bias binding is the usual way to finish quilts and blankets. So, the technique makes a great, thirty-minute baby blanket. Simply take a piece of fleece, two pieces of cotton fabric (wrong sides together) or a piece of corduroy and a piece of cotton (wrong sides together), and then use the exact same technique you've used to bind your place mat, folding at the corner, and join the edges at the bottom.

REVERSIBLE TOTE
WITH A FLAT BOTTOM

XXXXXXXXXXXXXXXXXXXXXXXXXXXXXXXXXXXXXXXXXXXXXXXX

Somewhere along the line in everyone's sewing experience, there is an epiphany moment, a big aha! So much of sewing is inside out and upside down, and wrapping your brain around the three-dimensionality of it all can take time and be daunting. This project consistently provides that moment of epiphany for my students. It's a chance to see how something that shouldn't work and doesn't make sense falls into place in the end. And suddenly so many patterns and designs become more understandable.

shopping list + supplies

Basic Sewing Tools
(see page 23)

½ yard (46cm) of fabric
for outside of bag

½ yard (46cm) of
coordinating fabric for
llining

matching thread

acrylic ruler

marking chalk

knitting needle (or other
turner)

skills you'll build

openings and
reversibles

linings

handles and straps

flat bottom techniques

109

Prepping the Pieces

When given the choice, I almost always prefer to line a project. It's so simple to just create what I envision, make a duplicate of it in another fabric, and then stitch them together. So neat, so tidy. That's what you'll be doing with this project, and for many new stitchers, this is a big aha! moment. It's a reminder that sewing is so often inside out and upside down, and seeing this tote go together can help all those three-dimensional ideas click in your head. That breakthrough really helps as you begin to design your own projects (yes, you!) in the future.

Begin by determining which of your two fabrics will be the outside of the bag and which will be the inside. Because the bag will be reversible, this is largely arbitrary, but it'll help with terminology as you go along. I'll consistently refer to the outside as "outside" and the inside as "lining."

Note: You can make a paper or cardboard pattern for this tote and might want to if you anticipate making a whole mess of them. I recommend making one tote to start, so that if you do find you want to tweak the design a bit, you can do so later and make a pattern then.

1. CUT FOUR THICKNESSES OF FABRIC

Because the pieces for this project are symmetrical, it's most efficient to cut the front and back of both the outside and lining simultaneously.

Fold the outside fabric with the right sides together; folding the fabric before cutting is referred to as "double thickness." Directly on top of that, lay your lining fabric in a double thickness, right sides together. You should to have four thicknesses now. Using your ruler, measure and mark 18" × 18" (46cm × 46cm) on the wrong side of the top-most fabric. Cut along these lines, keeping as straight as possible.

When Measurements Don't Really Matter

One of the great things about this tote is that the measurements aren't absolute. You can easily adapt the size to fit anything you'd like to put in it! I've made these to fit those awkwardly shaped library books from the kids' section, or to take my sewing supplies with me to class and to use as gift bags. Use this rule of thumb: Cut the body of the bag square if you plan to give it a flat bottom, and cut the straps the same length as one side, but skinnier. This will keep the proportions balanced. Obviously, if you prefer longer or shorter straps, adjust away! The point here is that the measurements are relative to what you want to achieve, and can easily be manipulated until you're happy.

Stitching the Bag

Making a lining is a simple matter of making another of your project, putting them right sides together and flipping them right side out after they're stitched. This tote is a great chance to practice that concept, and the clean, straight lines will help keep the work simple.

1. STITCH OUTSIDE TOGETHER IN U SHAPE

Place the two pieces for the outside of your bag with the right sides together and all edges even. Pin together, if desired. Stitch three sides to create a U shape (see Fig. 1 below) using a ½" (1.3cm) seam allowance.

2. STITCH LINING TOGETHER IN L SHAPE

Place the two pieces for the lining with the right sides together and all edges even. Pin together, if desired. On the lining pieces, stitch three sides, but rather than a U shape, create two L shapes with the short legs facing one another (see Fig. 2 below). This creates an opening for your hand when turning the bag right side out later.

When you stitch the edge with the short legs, you can do a little trick to skip over the opening in the bottom without removing the work from the machine. Get to the end of the stitch line, backtack, move forward to where you want the next stitches to begin, backtack there and continue stitching—no cutting required. This saves a little bit of time and will make you feel like a champ.

Fig. 1
Stitching diagram for outside

Fig. 2
Stitching diagram for lining

3. CLIP CORNERS

Cut off the two corners at the bottom of the outside and lining. Cutting, or clipping, the corners removes bulk and makes for a neater corner (see the sidebar below for more detail).

Clipping Corners and Curves

When projects have corners or curves, it's important to remove them (called clipping). This removes the bulk of the fabric to allow the finished project to lie smoothly.

CLIPPING CORNERS

For corners, clip the point to remove excess fabric that would prevent you from getting a sharp tip when your project is turned right side out.

CLIPPING CURVES

For curves, clip notches into the curve to allow the fabric to overlap along the curved edge, rather than lumping up and ruining a nice, smooth, rounded edge when you're done sewing.

Applying Flat-Bottom Techniques

To make the bag flat on the bottom, you'll use a super simple technique that requires only a few stitches.

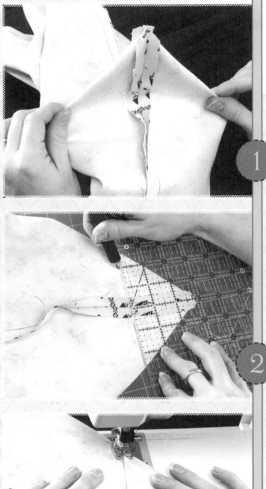

1. MAKE TRIANGLE AT BOTTOM OF BAG

With right sides together, take one bottom corner of the outside of your bag. Pull the front and back apart so the point makes a triangle.

2. DRAW CHALK LINE

Press this triangle down until the side seam touches the seam along the bottom of the bag. These two seams must align to create a clean look!

Draw a straight line 3" (8cm) from the triangle point from front to back across the seams, creating a triangle at the side of the bag. (By the way, altering the size of the triangle will alter the depth of the bag and change the overall dimensions. Feel free to play and bit and experiment!)

3. STITCH ALONG CHALK LINE

Stitch along the chalk line you've drawn. Keep the seam allowances open and flat as you stitch.

Repeat steps 1–3 on the other corner, making sure your triangles are the same size. Then repeat again on both corners of your lining. Remember: Your lining must be a mirror image of your outside if they're going to fit inside one another.

4. TRIM EXCESS FABRIC AND PRESS

Trim off the excess fabric, leaving about a ¼" (6mm) seam allowance. Press the corner. Voilà! A flat bottom to your bag.

113

Making the Handles

The handles for this bag are designed to be simple. There are multiple ways to create these (are you starting to notice that's true in a lot of sewing?), and I'll show you three. For this project, feel free to choose whichever method appeals to you most.

STRAP LENGTH

You'll need a different number of strap pieces in different widths, depending on the method you choose. But the length for each piece will be the same (18" [46cm]). (FYI, the length of the straps should be equal to the length of the side that will be longer when the bag is finished. This allows the overall dimensions of the bag to balance: The bottom two-thirds of the bag is the body, and the upper third are the handles.

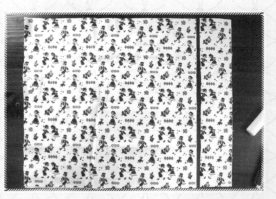

METHOD #1: OUTSIDE SEAM

This method is quick and simple because you don't have to take time to turn it inside out. This is also nice if you want to go for a skinnier strap that wouldn't permit you to turn it right side out. However, this method allows you only one fabric and has the distinct disadvantage of leaving visible stitching on the outer edge of each strap.

1. FOLD EDGES OF HANDLE PIECE

Cut two handles from the same fabric as the outside of your bag. The pieces should be 3" (8cm) wide (double the width of the finished handle).

Next, fold up both long edges on each of the handle pieces ½" (1.3cm) and press.

2. STITCH HANDLE

Fold the handle in half lengthwise with the wrong sides together. Stitch down the long side close to the folded edges. Repeat with the other handle. When you're finished stitching, press the handles flat.

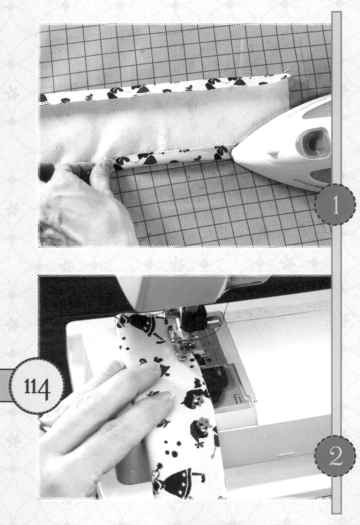

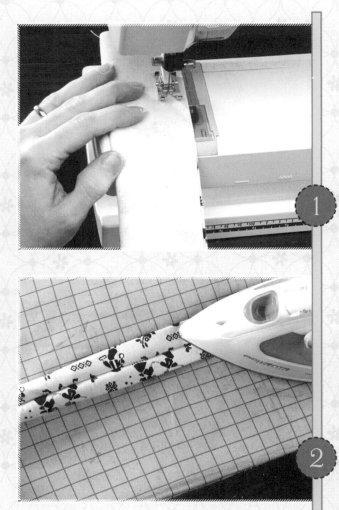

METHOD #2: HIDDEN SEAM

This method has the advantage of hiding the seam and making a more professional appearance than the other two methods, but again, it only allows you to use a single fabric.

1. FOLD IN HALF AND STITCH

Cut two straps from the same fabric as the outside of your bag. The pieces should be 3" (8cm) wide (double the width of the finished strap).

Fold one piece in half lengthwise, right sides together. Stitch a ½" (1.3cm) seam allowance along the long edge. Repeat with the other strap.

2. PRESS STRAP

Turn each strap right side out. (For tips on using a knitting needle to make the process easier, see the next page.) Press the straps with the seam in the center (which will go on the underside when you attach the straps to the bag).

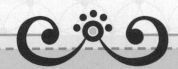

Speed It Up!

Here's a neat trick, as long as we're at it: chain stitching. When I make these bags, I tend to make them assembly-line style, one after another, so I have plenty on hand. That means I make all the outsides, then all the insides and then all the straps. As I'm working on the straps, rather than take each one off the machine and clip thread, put the next on the machine and start over, I put them under the presser foot one after another without removing the previous strap.

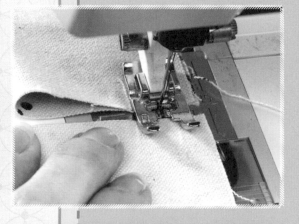

CHAIN STITCH STRAPS

Stitch one strap all the way to the end but don't backtack. Now place the next strap under the presser foot just in front of the strap you've just finished (but not overlapping the fabric—you don't want to stitch them to each other!). Begin stitching the next strap, and repeat over and over until you've finished them all. They'll be attached to one another by a short chain of stitches—just cut these stitches to separate the straps.

METHOD #3: REVERSIBLE

The advantage of this method is that it gives you a completely reversible strap, making the bag truly reversible. The other methods don't do that. The disadvantage is that with this method, the seams are clearly visible along the sides of the straps, and some folks don't like the way that looks. This is the method I used to make the straps for this bag.

1. CUT AND STITCH FABRIC PIECES

Cut four pieces for the straps: two of each of your two fabrics. They should be 1½" (4cm) wide.

Take a piece of the outside fabric and a piece of lining fabric; place the right sides together and match up the edges. Stitch along both long sides with a ½" (1.3cm) seam allowance. Repeat for the other strap.

2. START TURNING STRAP RIGHT SIDE OUT

Turn the straps right side out. With thin pieces like this, I like to use a knitting needle (you can also use an unsharpened pencil). It has a rounded end that slips right through the tube and makes it simple to turn right side out. Begin by turning just the tip of the strap right side out. Place the rounded end of the knitting needle under the fold and gently push upward.

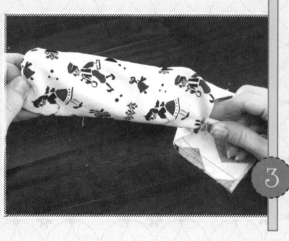

3. CONTINUE TURNING STRAP RIGHT SIDE OUT

Continue pushing the needle into the fabric and pulling the fabric out at the top. You'll feel the longer portion of the strap pushing up inside the opening, and you'll be able to gradually flip the whole tube right side out.

Press the straps flat with the seams at the edges.

Attaching the Handles and Lining

Regardless of which method you choose to create your handles, you should end up with two of them: one for each side of the bag. Now it's time to put them in place—bear with me on this one, because it makes some folks a little uncertain. Trust me and I'll get you there, I promise.

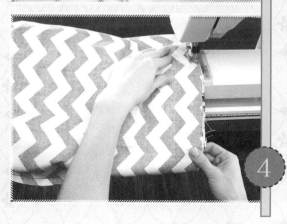

1. PIN HANDLES TO BAG

Turn the outside of the bag right side out. Pin one handle in place with each end of the handle about 4" (10cm) from the side seams of the bag. Pin the handle so the raw ends of the handle are even with the raw upper edge of the bag, and the right sides are together. The handle will make a U shape. If you've used Method #3 of handle construction, you'll want to be sure that the fabric that matches the outside of the bag is right sides together with the outside of the bag. Repeat to attach the second handle to the other side.

2. PLACE OUTSIDE OF BAG INSIDE LINING

With the lining of the bag wrong side out, take the entire outside-and-handles assembly (from step 1) and place it inside the bag lining. (Yes, I know, it seems as though this is a crazy thing to do, because you want the handles on the outside of the finished bag, where you can, like, use them, right? They totally will be—hang in there.)

3. MATCH SIDE SEAMS

Match your side seams on the outside and lining. (This part is really important, and is a common instruction in commercial patterns: "match side seams." People might not notice if your bag is slightly asymmetrical or imperfect, but they'll notice if your side seams aren't lined up.) Pin at those side seams and throw in another pin or two on each side, just to keep everything in place.

4. STITCH UPPER EDGE OF BAG

Now stitch all the way around the upper edge. (That's right, you heard me—all the way around. "Won't that close the bag up and trap the handles inside?" you ask. Stick it out, there, grasshopper.)

The easiest way to do this is to remove the table on your machine and expose the free arm. With the free arm exposed, smaller items like cuffs and hems fit neatly around the work space and make your stitching easier.

Finishing the Job

This is the exciting part where you get to melt your mind a little: turning the bag right side out. Remember how you sandwiched the handles between the outside and lining of the bag? And how that felt wrong because how are you going to get to the handles? This is where it all begins to make sense.

1. TURN BAG RIGHT SIDE OUT

Reach through the opening you left in the bottom of the lining. Grab the outer bag with the handles and pull it through the opening. Keep pulling until the whole bag is right side out. See how instead of being trapped inside, the handles are actually stitched between the two layers? Cool, huh?

2. STITCH LINING CLOSED

Now pull the lining out of the bag and press the bottom edge. Then put the bag on the machine, making sure only the lining is at the throat plate. In the small opening, fold under the edges so they match up with the other edges of the lining. Stitch the opening closed very, very close to the edge. (For an even cleaner finish, you can hand-stitch at the opening, making a truly reversible bag with an invisible closure. See pages 126–127 for the instructions.)

3. PRESS EDGES

Put the lining back inside the bag, and press all the way around the upper opening for a clean finish.

4. TOPSTITCH UPPER EDGE

At the upper edge of the bag stitch ¼" (6mm) away and parallel to the edge all the way around. This will keep the lining in place and give the bag a little more structure. Plus, it can add a little pizzazz to your tote. Consider using one of your fancy specialty stitches to make it extra special if you like!

FOR MORE INSPIRATION

One of my favorite things about this project is how adaptable it is. I can alter the dimensions in almost any way, adjust the strap length, add embellishments and sauce it up. Here are just a few ideas (left to right): add a ruffle and adorable outer pocket; add a flap; embroider or appliqué the outside of the bag. You can also add inner pockets and key fobs for added practicality. Or just skip the flat-bottom step altogether to make a simple gift bag (two gifts in one!).

I love the simplicity of the stitch-a-triangle flat-bottom technique, but sometimes you want a little more structure or sophistication to your tote. In that case, cut a separate rectangle to act as the bottom of your bag. Place a side seam of the outside of your bag at the center of the short side of your rectangle and pin in place. Do the same on the other short side of the rectangle with the other side seam. Now stitch all the way around all four sides, pivoting at each corner. Clip the corners, and you've made a cute little flat bottom to the bag! You can easily add piping or trim in the seam to dress it up. Keep in mind, though, just how much of your bag's width gets eaten up by the sides of the bag bottom, and plan accordingly. So, for example, if my front and back are both 18" (46cm) wide, and I want my bottom panel to be 6" (15cm) deep, I lose 3" (8cm) on the right and left of the bag, making my bottom panel 12" × 6" (30cm × 15cm) in order to fit properly.

RELAXING EYE MASK
WITH CURVES

XXXXXXXXXXXXXXXXXXXXXXXXXXXXXXXXXXXXXXXXXXXXXXXXXXXXXXX

Few things seem quite as indulgent as an eye mask, a luxury we can only use when lying down, with our eyes closed, preferably listening to relaxing music. One of my favorite things about sewing is the ability it gives me to make fantastic, quick, easy gifts; I usually make a bunch assembly-line style to prepare for Christmas, and then I have a few leftover for myself! This project is fantastic whether you give it away or pop it in the bedside table for the next time you have a moment to breathe.

shopping list + supplies

Basic Sewing Tools
(see page 23)

pattern (printed and cut)
for the Relaxing Eye
Mask, found on book CD

one fat quarter of quilt-
weight cotton or cotton
flannel (this can be two
different prints if you'd
like your eye pillow to be
reversible, and you can
totally use scraps)

matching thread

knitting needle (or other
turner)

2 cups of dried lentils or
split peas

1 cup of dried lavender
flowers, rose petals,
lemongrass—something
yummy!

sheet of cardstock or
printer paper

hand sewing needle

skills you'll build

stitching curves

insides and outsides

making ties

filling and stuffing

slip stitch

121

Sewing Curves

Alright, you've mastered stitching straight lines at this point, and you're well in the habit of backtacking. Now, it's time to master stitching curves. Stitching a curved line is in some ways a totally different ball of wax, but in others, it's really just more of the same. The key lies in watching your seam allowance as you work.

Now's the time to put all of that abstract stitching practice to good use: Remember when we went over the Driver's Ed Theory of Sewing? Well, this is the road test. You'll be great—no parallel parking or anything! The important part to keep in mind as you create curves is that the smoother your stitch line on the inside, the smoother your shape on the outside. When you turn your work right side out, any jagged stitches will result in a lumpy seam, and you want the end result to be as pretty as you can get it.

Sloppy versus smooth stitching

The photos on the left show how sloppy stitching results in a jagged curve. The photos on the right show how taking your time to create smooth stitches along a curve results in lovely curved edges.

Stitch Tip

If you feel you're really struggling to keep your stitch straight (or curved), consider adding a piece of masking or painter's tape at the seam allowance guide line on the throat plate. This will give you a longer line as a reference for your sewing.

Making Ties

In order to keep the mask on for relaxing, you need some ties. You'll want them to lie nice and flat so you'll have a comfortable relaxation experience. (Just like with the tote's handles, these straps can be made any number of ways.)

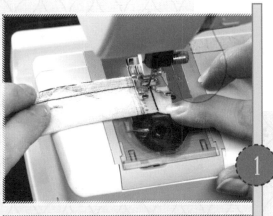

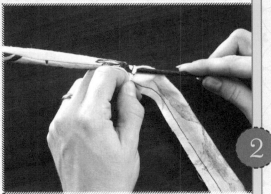

1

CUT OUT FABRIC PIECES

Cut the pieces for this project using the pattern. Fold the fat quarter in half with the wrong sides together and set the fold line of the pattern piece along the folded fabric edge. Pin in place (or use pattern weights) and cut out. Repeat on different fabric for a reversible mask, or cut another from the same fabric. You now have a front and back. (For more detailed information on pinning and cutting patterns, see pages 176–177.)

Then cut out the tie pieces. Cut one tie 1½" × 9" (4cm × 23cm) and the other tie 1½" × 14" (4cm × 36cm). (You'll notice that one tie is longer than the other. That's so the mask will tie to one side. What's relaxing about a knot on the back of your noggin?)

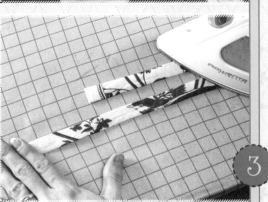

2

1. STITCH TIES

Fold each tie in half lengthwise with the right sides together. Make sure the raw edges line up. Stitch a seam along the long edge, using the edge of your presser foot as a seam guide. Pivot at the corner and stitch the short end.

2. TURN TIES RIGHT SIDE OUT

Turn the ties right side out. For a refresher on this step, flip back to the handles on the tote bag on page 116.

3

3. PRESS TIES FLAT

Press the ties flat, with the seam in the center, which will be the underside when stitched onto the mask.

123

Tie Variations

There's nothing that says you have to fasten this puppy with fabric ties! Why not try ribbons, rickrack or a braided strap instead? Just attach it the same way you would the fabric ties.

Stitching the Parts Together

Stitching curves, as I've said before, is really the same principle as stitching straight lines: It's all about keeping an eye on that seam allowance and maintaining consistency. Remember, the smoother your stitches here, the prettier your finished results will be.

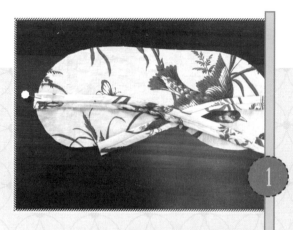

1. PIN TIES TO MASK

Place the ties on the dots as indicated on the sleep mask pattern. Lay each so the length of the tie is on the front of the mask. The raw ends of the ties should be even with the raw edges of the mask and with seams facing up.

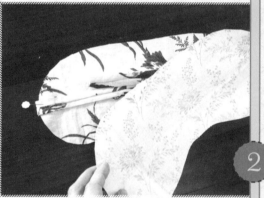

2. PLACE BACK PIECE OVER TOP

Place the back side of the mask over the top of the front piece with the right sides together, sandwiching the ties between them.

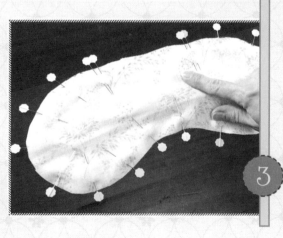

3. PIN MASK PIECES TOGETHER

Pin around the outer edge of the mask leaving an opening for turning. I like to use double pins at each side of my opening to be to create a visual reminder to stop and start at those spots and avoid stitching the entire circumference of the mask shut. I left about three finger widths for my opening.

Make sure the pins holding the ties stay on the outside of the mask.

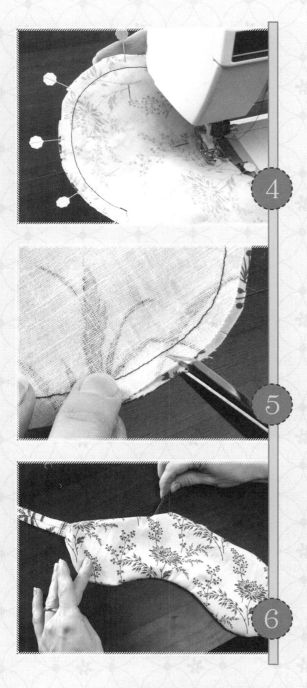

4. STITCH MASK WITH OPENING

Stitch around the curves of the mask with a ⅜" (1cm) seam allowance. Remember to watch that seam guide closely, and aim to keep the edge of your fabric consistently against that line as you go. Start slowly and take your time!

Be sure to leave the opening (for turning your work right side out) unstitched.

5. CLIP CURVES

Around the curved edges of the eye mask, clip into the seam allowance up to, but not through, the stitching to reduce the bulk when you turn it right side out. (See the sidebar on page 112 for details.)

6. SMOOTH OUT CURVES

Here's another place where I just love using my knitting needle. After you turn your eye mask right side out, use the pointed end of the knitting needle to ride along the inside of the seam and smooth it out. Then press the fabric to make those edges nice and clean. You'll get fewer weird folds and overlaps, and have a bigger mask to really block out the light.

Filling

Before tackling the filling, decide what kind of eye mask you'd like (see sidebar below). Mix your selections together in a small bowl and then fill up the mask.

1. FILL MASK

A funnel comes in handy for this step, but I tend to make one on the fly out of a rolled-up bit of printer paper or cardstock. Place the end of your funnel in the opening you've left along one edge of the eye mask. Slowly pour the mixture into the eye mask. The beans will accumulate at the bottom and make it fat, but you're probably going to need more than you expect in order to get good coverage once your mask is on. It feels a little odd to lie back and have all the filling at the edges, so overfill rather than underfill at this step.

After all the filling is in, allow it to fall to one side away from the opening you've left. Brush any stray bits out of the way.

Filling Options

The various scents and effects of different fillings can make your eye mask truly unique and give you options for gifts for various occasions! Here are just a few, but go nuts when making up your own. Mix about one cup of the scented filling with two cups of lentils or split peas.

Relaxing: lavender and chamomile
Invigorating: rosemary and lemongrass
Romantic: rose petals and orange peel

Finishing With a Slip Stitch

When the filling is in, it's time to close up the mask. I'll show you how to do a hand-sewn slip stitch to make it pretty, but you can also stitch the opening shut just as you did to the opening in the lining of your tote bag (see page 118). The slip stitch is a simple, clean finish that looks great on the inside and outside of projects. It's a pretty common stitch to use to make the inside of a garment look couture and complete, and it is a fantastic skill to have in your skill set.

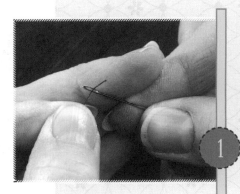

1. THREAD NEEDLE

Pick up a hand sewing needle. Thread the eye with a single thread. Then pull the thread all the way to the end and tie a knot to keep the end of the thread from slipping through the needle.

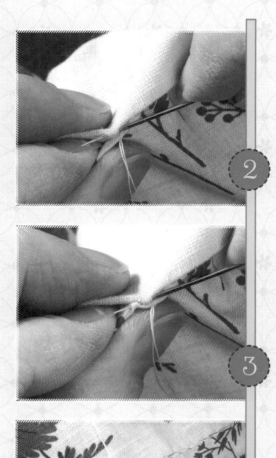

2. START STITCHING

Fold under the raw edges of the fabric and hold the opening closed. Insert the needle on the inside of the opening.

3. CONTINUE STITCHING

Bring the needle through the fold on one side and then through the fold on the opposite side. Repeat, creating nearly invisible stitches as you go.

4. KNOT WHEN FINISHED

When you complete your stitching, tie a simple knot at the end and make sure it's up close to the fabric. Add a second knot on top of it and you're done.

There, now. Don't you feel more relaxed already? You can use these techniques to make simple round pillows, small stuffed animals, almost anything with filling and a curved edge. You're so boss.

POWER PHRASE #2

66 IT'S A PROTOTYPE 99

Not perfect the first time? Avoid the temptation to beat yourself up and toss it aside. You've never done this before, for heaven's sake! Allow some imperfections at first, and remember that no project you create is the last project you'll create. Imperfections often add value and interest and remind us of why we love handmade. If you're addicted to perfection, mistakes also reveal how not to do something. Think of it as the Thomas Edison approach to sewing. You didn't ruin it or do it wrong, you just found a way that didn't produce the results you desire. And that's cool, because there's going to be a next time.

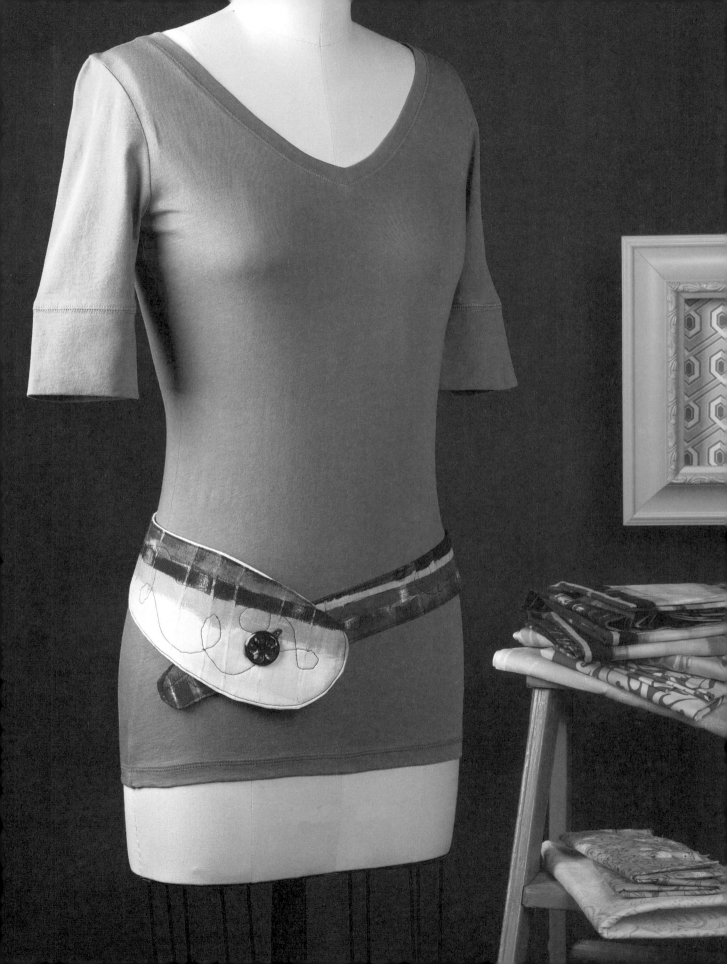

HIPSTER BELT
WITH BUTTON CLOSURE

Ah, closure! We're all after a little bit of it. In this case, we're looking to make closures for our projects. The two primary closures in sewing are buttons and zippers. Some find that they prefer one over the other—totally fine. No one's going to get any feelings hurt if you decide you're more of a zipper person than a button person. Let's try a little of each, and you can determine which appeals to you more! Let's start here with a button project, and then tackle the zipper project.

This belt is kicky and modern, and has a funky shape that goes with everything—plus it'll give you a chance to work on your buttonhole skills.

shopping list + supplies

Basic Sewing Tools (see page 23)

pattern (printed and cut) for the Hipster Belt, found on book CD

½ yard (69cm) of fabric

½ yard (46cm) of heavy-weight sew-in interfacing (such as Peltex or Timtex)

matching thread

contrasting thread

marking chalk

buttonhole foot

large sew-on button

seam ripper (optional)

knitting needle or other turner

• • •

skills you'll build
free-motion quilting

buttonholes and buttons

129

Preparing and Attaching the Fabric and Interfacing

Interfacing is used to give weight and stiffness to projects. You'll see it in the base of handbags to give them shape, in collars and cuffs to help them wear better and longer, and behind buttonholes to give the stitches some support. For this project, you'll place interfacing between the fabric layers to give your belt some weight.

CUT OUT FABRIC AND INTERFACING PIECES

Notice that the pattern has two lines: an outer fabric cutting line and an inner dashed line. When cutting the interfacing, use the dashed line. You can either cut off the outer edge to make the pattern smaller (and reprint it the next time you want to make the belt) or print two versions and trim one to interfacing size. Just take care to cut the fabric larger than the interfacing.

Lay the fabric in a double thickness and the interfacing in a single thickness. Pin the pattern pieces to the fabric and interfacing and cut them out. (For more detailed information on pinning and cutting with patterns, see pages 176–177.) You should end up with six pieces: left and right front pieces, left and right back pieces, and left and right interfacing. Using marking chalk, transfer the pattern markings for the opening and buttonhole placement to the wrong side of the fabric.

1. STITCH LEFT AND RIGHT PIECES TOGETHER

To conserve fabric, I created the pattern with left and right pieces for both the front and back of the belt. So first you need to stitch those two pieces together to make one long piece.

Place the straight edges of the left and right front pieces with the right sides together. Stitch the center back seam using a ¼" (6mm) seam allowance. Do the same with the two back pieces and the two interfacing pieces.

2. PRESS SEAM ALLOWANCES

Press open the seam allowance on the front, back and interfacing pieces.

3. STITCH FRONT AND BACK TOGETHER

Place the front and back pieces right sides together. Stitch around the outer edge using a ½" (1.3cm) seam allowance. Make sure to match the center back seams as you stitch.

As you stitch, leave an opening between the two dots shown on the pattern piece (so you'll be able to turn the belt right side out later), and backtack at either end of that opening.

4. CLIP CURVES

Clip the curves of the edges of the belt. Then turn the belt right side out.

5. PRESS BELT FLAT

Smooth out the curves from the inside, making sure that the seam lies flat all the way around the perimeter of the belt. Take it to the ironing board and press it flat.

6. INSERT INTERFACING INTO BELT

Slide the interfacing in through the opening you've left in the belt, to fit into the interior "pocket" with the tail end first. You might have to wrestle it a bit to get it into the tighter ends, but keep trying—it'll happen!

(In many cases, the interfacing is attached to one fabric piece prior to stitching fronts and backs together, but here, I wanted to avoid some of the bulk. You'll get a chance to do that when we get to one of the varsity lessons, so sit tight!)

Once the interfacing is in place, turn under the raw edges of the opening and press.

Sewing Contrast Stitches

Contrast stitching involves using thread of a different color than your fabric in order to create a visible line of stitches. In this case, you'll do some contrast topstitching around the edge of the belt to give it some oomph. Contrast stitches are always more visible— they're supposed to be because that's what they're for. Take your time, though, because a contrast thread is more likely to reveal inconsistencies than a matching thread will.

TOPSTITCH PERIMETER OF BELT

Using the edge of your presser foot as a guide, topstitch around the entire outer edge, starting at the center back and catching the opening closed. Be sure the folded-under edges at the opening line up as you stitch them shut. Your stitches should go through both fabrics and the interfacing, and will hold everything in place.

Free-Motion Quilting (for Super Beginners)

Free-motion quilting is a lot like thread drawing, except it goes through multiple layers of fabric and binds them together. You'll be using this technique to add another layer of visual interest to your belt, again with contrast thread.

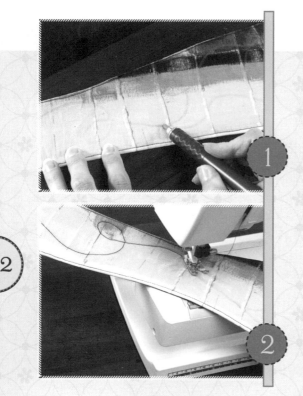

1. DRAW STITCH LINES IN CHALK

In chalk, draw lines for stitching on the front side of the belt. You'll stitch directly on top of these, but sketch them lightly enough that you'll be able to remove them later.

Choose a contrast thread—it can be the same as the thread you used to topstitch or another color altogether. Maybe try some of the cool variegated threads on the market, which change colors every few inches as you stitch, or a thicker machine embroidery or metallic thread that has a bit more visual presence.

2. STITCH OVER CHALK LINES

Lower your feed dogs, if you're able, to give you total control over your stitching. (Some models even come with a special free-motion presser foot that gives you plenty of visibility and allows you to turn on a dime.) Stitch directly on top of your guidelines from one end of the belt to the other.

Making Buttonholes

For this belt, you're not going to use a buckle or ring: You're adding a button! (By the way, this entire project can easily be resized to become a choker necklace or a wrist cuff, and buttons look great on all of them.) Here, you'll be adding a button closure for a very cool finish.

There are conventions for the placement of buttonholes on most projects, most of them focusing on the fact that folks like them more or less centered. For this project, you should be less concerned about buttonholes being centered than about the belt really fitting you. Because these buttons will be stationary, the belt won't be adjustable later, so you want to mark them properly now.

Up first is stitching the buttonhole. The following instructions assume you have a four-step buttonhole (because that is the most common). Other types of buttonhole functions will work differently—check the sidebar on page 136 to see which description most closely matches your machine, and alter your steps accordingly.

1. MARK BUTTON PLACEMENT

Wrap the belt around your waist the way you'd like it to hang. Use chalk to mark where the button (on the smaller tail) should go.

Then mark the length of your button where you've marked the buttonhole. Use short lines to indicate the buttonhole length. Don't make your buttonhole exactly the same size as the button; make it slightly larger, or it'll just get stuck and you'll get frustrated.

Better Buttonholes

Your best bet for good results when making buttonholes is to stitch a couple practice rounds first on a piece of scrap fabric so you'll know what to expect. Keep in mind that most machines give you arrows on the icons on your machine front to remind you when to do what, so you won't have to memorize all of the steps right away.

Some folks find that their machine stitches the left and right zigzag at different lengths, making their buttonhole slightly lopsided. Or maybe you like a darker stitch on your buttonhole. You can always go around a second time and stitch right on top of the first buttonhole, as long as you haven't opened it up yet. Check to see if your machine requires you to reset your buttonhole function first, though, by dialing away from the buttonhole stitches and back to standard stitches, then selecting the buttonhole stitches again. Some machines will make a "thunk" sound when you do this, indicating that the machine recognizes the end of one buttonhole and the beginning of the next. If yours is one of these, you'll need to do that each time you stitch a buttonhole. If you don't, when you begin your second buttonhole, you'll just keep stitching a straight line into oblivion.

2. ALIGN UP CHALK LINES IN BUTTONHOLE FOOT

Remove the machine's standard foot and replace it with the buttonhole foot. Place the belt under the buttonhole foot, lining up the chalk lines inside the "window" in the foot. Check your machine to see if it sews Step 1 away from you or toward you (most have an icon or image on the front of the machine that indicates which way to stitch first). Depending on which way your machine sews, align one of the short chalk lines (which will become the bar tacks when the buttonhole is stitched) between the grooves or red marks you see at the top of the buttonhole foot. Check your owner's manual to be sure, or run some practice buttonholes on scrap fabric until you feel comfortable with how your machine will behave.

3. COMPLETE FIRST SIDE AND FIRST BAR TACK

Step 1 on most four-step machines involves stitching the zigzag at one long side of the buttonhole (either toward you or away from you). So, start stitching and begin making your first bar tack, and watch the mark you've made in chalk on your fabric to determine when to stop stitching. Look for the other bar tack chalk line to appear in the "window" on the foot. Avoid stitching too far by using the grooves or red marks in the side of the buttonhole foot as a gauge for when your mark is coming up.

After Step 1 is done, move your buttonhole function on the machine to Step 2, the bar tack. Stitch side to side four or five times and then stop and prep for Step 3.

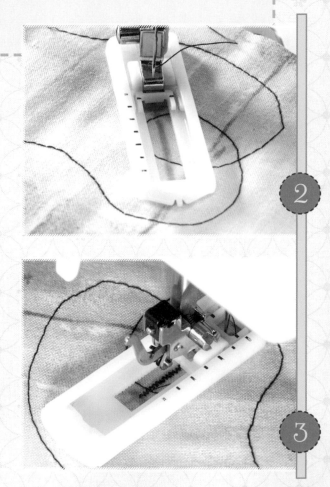

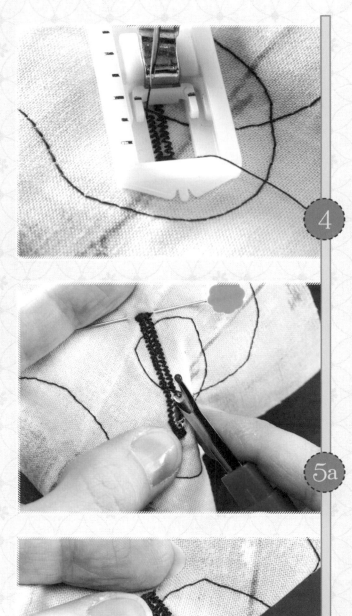

4. COMPLETE SECOND SIDE AND BAR TACK

Step 3 is really the same as Step 1, just on the other side and headed in the opposite direction. Stitch down until you get to the other end of your buttonhole, again using the guides on the side of the buttonhole foot to alert you when to stop. Switch to Step 4 and stitch the other bar tack. You're done! (It was easier than you thought, right?)

5. OPEN BUTTONHOLE

OPTION A: RIPPING OPEN

One way to open up the buttonhole is to use a seam ripper. First, place a pin at one end, through the bar tack, to ensure that you don't go too far. (I did that once, and my mom was so not pleased.) Using the pointed end of the seam ripper, pierce the space between your two rows of zigzags at one end, close to the bar tack. Get the U-shaped part down to the fabric and use its sharp edge to slice between but not through the threads, all the way to the other end. (After they're cut open, that's where your buttonhole lives forever, so do take care here.)

OPTION B: CUTTING OPEN

Alternately, you can use the old-school method of opening your buttonhole. Fold the buttonhole in half, matching the bar tacks. Snip the center with sharp scissors and then unfold it and continue clipping until the whole buttonhole is cut open.

Variations on a Buttonhole

Manual Buttonhole

This is the old-school buttonhole, as in you make it all by yourself. A machine that makes manual buttonholes asks you to install the zigzag stitches and bar tacks with no assistance from the machine; my 1969 Singer was like this. The key to keep in mind is that the bar tacks at either end of your buttonhole should be twice the width of each row of zigzag stitch.

One-Step Buttonhole

A one-step machine allows you to lower a lever at the back of the needle bar that interacts with your buttonhole foot to indicate when to change directions while making the buttonhole. You'll have a large, white plastic buttonhole foot and a lever behind your needle (usually to the left) with an icon of a buttonhole on it. Attach the buttonhole foot and lower the lever so it fits between the two catches on the left side of the foot. At the back of the foot is a space to place your button to tell the machine what size hole to make. Lower your buttonhole foot onto your fabric and stitch! This style of buttonhole foot is most common with newer, computerized machines, which usually give you a selection of four or six styles of buttonhole to create.

Automatic Buttonhole

Probably the least common type of buttonholer on the market, this is a special attachment that works with computerized machines. When you connect the foot to the machine, the computer is able to change directions at the appropriate time for the size buttonhole you select. You get to pick the color of thread.

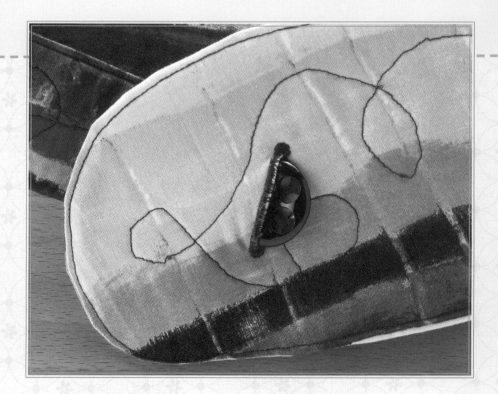

Attaching Buttons by Machine

Of course, you can always attach buttons by hand, but the day I learned my machine would do it, I actually teared up—no exaggeration here. Some newer machines come with a special foot that allows you to stitch on a button, but you can also use your zigzag function and standard presser foot.

STITCH BUTTON

Replace the buttonhole foot with the standard presser foot or, if you have one, a button foot. Place your belt on the throat plate with the right side up. Place the button on the button placement chalk mark you made earlier. Set your machine to a stitch length of zero—no forward movement—and adjust the stitch width until the needle goes cleanly in each hole of the button. Lower your presser foot to pinch the button to the fabric. Zigzag between two holes, then remove from the machine and tie a knot!

The advantage of using the button foot is that it makes a little shank and gives the button more room to maneuver. To mimic that, try placing a toothpick or T-pin on top of the button when you place it under the presser foot and then stitch over it.

Stitch Tip

For the most professional look, match the thread color you use to attach your button to the button, rather than to the fabric. This will make those little thread loops disappear, and your buttons, not the thread color, will pop visually.

PIPED THROW PILLOW
WITH A UNIVERSAL ZIPPER

Attaching zippers seems to be one of those intimidating sewing tasks that folks put off learning to do. But zippers are so easy that once you learn to install one you'll wonder what all the fuss was about! The same thing is true for piping: We all want to know how to add some pizzazz to our projects, but trim can look scary and hard to manage. This project lets you do both in one place and without any of the headache you thought you'd find. Plus, you'll learn how to join two pieces of fabric invisibly on an edge and cover all the basic pillow skills you're likely to ever need. Woo-hoo!

shopping list + supplies

Basic Sewing Tools (see page 23)

½ yard (46cm) of main fabric for body of pillow

2 yards (1.8m) of continuous bias tape 2" (5cm) wide in contrasting fabric

rotary cutter, cutting mat and acrylic ruler

2 yards (1.8m) of piping cord, ⅜" (1cm) width

16" (41cm) polyester/universal zipper to match main fabric

matching thread

16" × 16" (41cm × 41cm) pillow form

½" (1.3cm) quilters tape

seam ripper

marking chalk

zipper foot

skills you'll build

installing universal zippers

making piping with bias tape

installing piping and trims

139

Cutting Out the Pillow: Just a Smidgen of Math

Pillows are addictive. They're quick and easy to make, and almost everybody can use another one. Or six. Knowing some basic guidelines will make constructing pillows simple. To get a fitted pillow cover, it needs to be the same size as the pillow form that you'll stuff inside it. So, for a 16" × 16" (41cm × 41cm) pillow form, you'd make a 16" × 16" (41cm × 41cm) pillow cover. For an overstuffed pillow, you want it to be an inch smaller all around than the pillow form (or 15" × 15" [38cm × 38cm]). For a loosely stuffed, Shabby Chic-style pillow, you'd need it an inch larger all around, or 17" × 17" (43cm × 43cm). For this project, let's focus on a fitted cover.

For this pillow, you're going make a fitted cover for a 16" × 16" (41cm × 41cm) pillow form. Before cutting your fabric, though, you have to add in seam allowances to get the 16" × 16" (41cm × 41cm) finished dimension; I usually use ½" (1.3cm), just because it makes the math easier. You'll want that seam allowance on both sides, not just one, so adding a seam allowance of ½" (1.3cm) means adding 1" (3cm) to each measurement. So that means you need to cut out squares for the front and back that measure 17" × 17" (43cm × 43cm). But wait! You're also putting in a zipper that runs through the center back of your pillow, and you'll need seam allowances on each side of the zipper, too. So for the back you need a piece that measures 17" tall × 18" wide (43cm × 46cm), right?

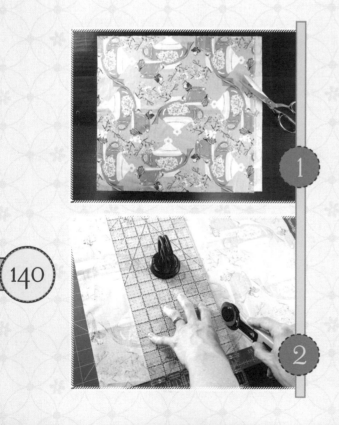

1. CUT OUT FRONT AND BACK PIECES

Rather than cut one piece on a single thickness that's 17" × 17" (43cm × 43cm) and a whole other piece on a single thickness that's 17" × 18" (43cm × 46cm), I think it's easier to cut two pieces the same size and then trim one of them down.

Start with the ½ yard (46cm) of fabric in a double thickness, right sides together. Mark with chalk 17" (43cm) tall by 18" (46cm) wide. (This is a good place to be thinking about the direction of your print: You'll want your zipper running top to bottom, so orient your fabric now to make the side-to-side measurement the 18" [46cm] one.) Cut through both thicknesses. Then cut 1" (3cm) off the piece that will be the pillow front.

2. MARK CUT LINE ON BACK

Set aside the front piece. Place the back piece right side down with the 18" (46cm) running horizontally. Use your ruler to measure the halfway point across the width (9" [23cm]) and cut down the center of the piece. This should divide your fabric into two sections, each measuring 17" × 9" (43cm × 23cm).

Stitching the Piping

Most of us own or have owned a sofa at some point. The vast majority of sofas are piped around the edges: that teeny, round cord that runs along the edge of cushions and sofa pillows. As a result, we all know more or less what piping is supposed to look like when it's done properly. So you're starting with the knowledge that because most all trims are applied in the same manner, once you've conquered one, you've got the skills to take on any of them.

For this project, you'll be creating your own custom piping using bias tape. The fullness of the piping is created by the filler cord you'll stuff inside it. Piping filler cord is usually found in the home decor section of the fabric store, either by the yard or in precut packages, and comes in a variety of widths. I love the look of the fat stuff, but I think the skinnier stuff is easier to work with the first time around.

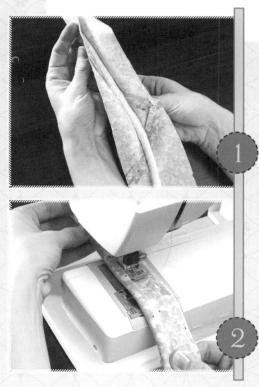

1. WRAP BIAS TAPE AROUND PIPING CORD

Place the piping cord inside the bias tape with the seams to the inside, wrong sides together. Wrap the bias tape around the piping cord and bring the raw edges of the bias tape together.

2. BASTE THE PIPING SHUT

Before placing the piping on the pillow, basting it together gives you a little more control. So switch to your machine's zipper foot. (Some machines come with a specialty piping foot, but that's pretty rare.) Set your machine to the basting stitch.

With the piping cord off to the left and the zipper foot set to the right, place the piping fabric beneath the zipper foot. Your goal here is to stitch as close to the cord as you can get to make the piping nice and snug. On many machines, you can adjust your needle to the right or left, which allows you to get super close to the needle. With the machine set to a straight stitch, try adjusting your stitch width and see if that doesn't cause your needle bar to move right or left of center, letting you get right up against that piping cord. Baste the entire length.

Store-Bought versus Custom-Made Piping Cord

Ready-made piping is available in most fabric stores. There's nothing wrong with this piping, but I tend to avoid it for three main reasons: One, it's always poly-cotton, and you know how I feel about artificial fibers (ick!); two, it comes in finite lengths, and I frequently need more than the length that comes in the package; and three, it only comes in solid colors (usually fewer than ten and three of them are pink). So, because piping is easy to make, using custom-made is a no-brainer for the good-taste-laden stitcher.

Zipper Feet and How They Roll

Snap-On Zipper Foot with Groove

Most newer machines use a snap-on system to attach their presser feet. For this version of the zipper foot, you'll probably have two bars, one on the left and one on the right. Snap the foot on so the needle is always closest to the side of the zipper you're stitching. Most of these also have a groove in the bottom of the foot that rides over the zipper teeth perfectly and keeps them in position; it's a good way to double-check that you've got your presser foot on the correct side of the zipper teeth.

Screw-On Zipper Foot with Slider

Some machines have a zipper foot that attaches with the screw at the side of the needle bar. These have an independent slider at the back that allows you to adjust the distance from the needle. Truthfully, this is my vast preference in zipper feet, because it can be used for a lot more than applying zippers. Remove your regular presser foot and screw this one into place. Adjust the back slider so the presser foot is on the opposite side of the needle from the zipper teeth; this gets the needle as close to the zipper teeth as possible.

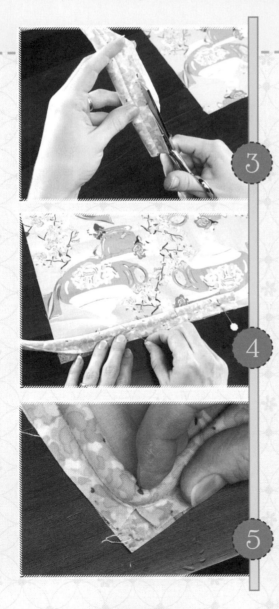

3. TRIM BIAS TAPE

Trim the seam allowance on the piping bias tape to ¼" (6mm).

4. PIN CORD ON PILLOW FRONT

Now you're ready to apply the piping to the front of the pillow (because there won't be a zipper there, it makes easier work for you).

Place the pillow front (the 17" × 17" [43cm × 43cm] piece) right side up. Beginning at the bottom, lay the piping's raw edges even with the edge of the pillow front. So, the piping should lie toward the inside of the pillow. Start with the end of the piping in the center of one edge (not at the corner). Pin the piping in place.

5. CUT INTO CORNERS

When you near each corner, you need to trim into the seam allowance of the piping to make a clean, 90-degree angle on the outside. To do so, measure the distance from the seam allowance to the corner point (in this case, it's ½" [1.3cm]) and clip into the piping. Now you can "break" the piping around the corner.

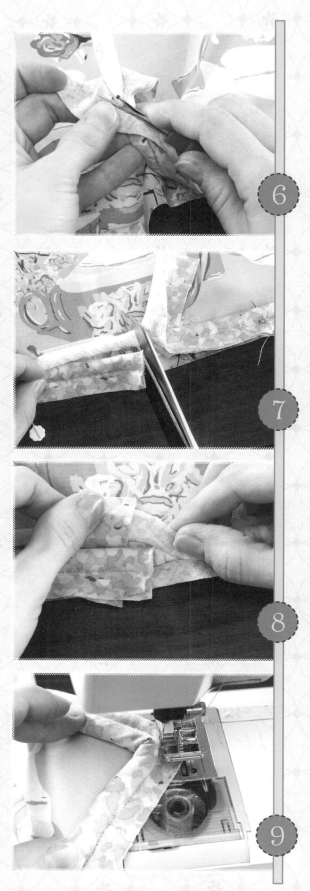

6. RIP OPEN END OF PIPING

When you get back to the first side, make sure the ends of your piping overlap by about 2" (5cm), which, by the way, is about three fingers wide. By joining the piping ends at the overlap, you will create the illusion in your finished pillow that there is a seamless line of piping all the way around, one with no beginning and no end. (It's kind of romantic, when you think about it, like a wedding ring.)

Start by removing the basting stitches on one end of the piping cord to expose the cording inside. It doesn't matter what end you chose, really. But to make things less confusing, open up the end on the right (the end you wrapped all around the pillow).

7. TRIM CORDING

Lay the two cording ends side by side. Trim the opened-up end (the right end) so the two ends butt up against one another without overlapping.

8. WRAP CORDING WITH OPEN BIAS TAPE

Fold under the end of the opened-up bias tape. Then wrap the uncovered cording (on the right side) and the covered cording (on the left side) with the opened-up bias tape. Pin it in place.

9. BASTE PIPING IN PLACE

With your zipper foot still on the machine and your stitches still set to basting, baste all the way around the piping, as close to the cord as you are able. This will hold the piping in place when you put it all together in a few steps.

Adding Zippers

Zippers are widely regarded as intimidating by many stitchers. These handy devices really don't deserve the bad rap, if you ask me, and can be quite simple to install. You'll be putting a zipper up the center back of your cushion and use a universal zipper (which usually says "polyester" on the package).

The universal zipper is the one you're most likely to use for things like pants or skirts with a waistband and hook-and-eye closure. They're easy to find in a variety of sizes and colors, and work for piles of projects. Learning to install the universal zipper is a little more complicated than the invisible, but because of its nearly limitless potential, it's where we'll start.

When faced with the racks of zippers in the store, if you have the choice between purchasing one that's the right length but the wrong color or one that's too long but the right color, always go with the one that's too long—you can make a zipper shorter (see the sidebar below), but you can't magically make it a different color. For now, I recommend refraining from using a zipper that's too short, since it's complicated to add a too-short zipper to a project. (But when you're ready to learn, see the sidebar on page 147.)

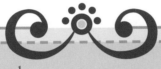

Shortening a Zipper

Zippers have three main parts: the zipper tape, which is made of polyester; the zipper pull, which moves the slider up and down along the teeth that are installed in the zipper tape; and the zip stop, which prevents the slider from falling off the end. To shorten a zipper, all you need to do is create a new zip stop at another, higher location.

1. Use your chalk to mark where on the zipper you'd like the new stop. Do this carefully, because after you stitch over the zipper teeth, they'll likely be bent, and the zipper won't zip past that point any longer.

2. With your feed dogs lowered, or with your stitch setting on zigzag and stitch length set to zero, stitch a series of zigzag stitches—four or five—over this mark. Cut off the excess zipper length. That's all there is to it!

1. BASTE BACK PIECES TOGETHER

Baste the two back pieces with the right sides together along center cut line. Press the seam allowances open.

2. PIN ZIPPER TO SEAM ALLOWANCE

Fold the back of the pillow in half with the right sides together, but with the seam allowances extended. Then set the open zipper face down on the pressed-open seam allowances—make sure it's face down, since you'll want to unzip from the outside later, not the inside. Each side of the zipper should go on each side of the seam allowance. Pin the zipper in place.

3. BASTE ZIPPER IN PLACE

Using your zipper foot and a basting stitch, stitch the right side of the zipper tape to the seam allowance. Make sure the zipper is stitched only to the seam allowance, and not the visible back of the pillow.

145

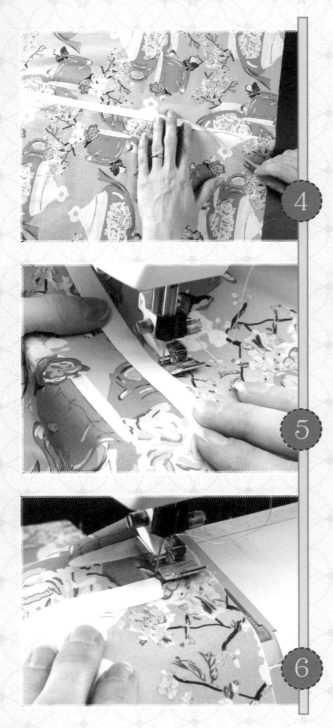

4. PLACE QUILTER'S TAPE OVER SEAM

Flip the back over so you can see the seam from the right side. And now, here's my favorite 1950s-era trick: Attach a piece of ½" (1.3cm) quilter's tape centered over the seam. This will guide your stitches in the next step. At the end of the zipper, feel around through the fabric for the metal zip stop. Rip your tape off just before it reaches the stop to indicate to yourself where not to stitch—remember, stitching over the metal zip stop will snap a needle and scare the crap out of you, so avoid it if you can.

5. STITCH SIDE OF ZIPPER

Place the back-and-zipper combo in the machine with the zipper foot at the edge of the tape. Using a regular stitch length (not a basting stitch), begin at the top and stitch all the way down that side of the zipper.

6. PIVOT AND STITCH OTHER SIDE

Remember to stop at the edge of the tape to avoid the zipper stop. Don't stop too short because where you stitch on the teeth is as far as the zipper will unzip. Pivot stitch across the zipper, then pivot again and head up the other side. (By the way, the zipper teeth are plastic and stitching across them won't hurt a bit.)

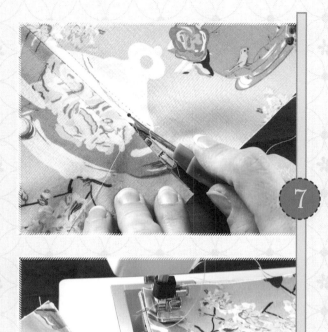

7. RIP OUT BASTING STITCHES

When you're finished stitching, remove the tape. Then use the seam ripper to remove all the basting stitches covering your zipper. Remember that the seam ripper is only sharp at the U part, and that pulling with the finger will snag your stitches.

8. STITCH TOP OF ZIPPER

Return to the upper end of the zipper, pull down the zipper pull, and complete the lines of stitches. This step is especially necessary if the shape of your zipper foot won't let you get close enough to the closed zipper pull to stitch all the way to the top without running off to the side and throwing stitches around willy-nilly. Just pull that zipper pull down enough to get it out of the way and then go back on the left and right to finish out the line of stitching all the way to the top.

Using a Too-Short Zipper

What happens if you find yourself with a zipper that's too short for the pillow you're making? No worries! You can stitch a box around the zipper and make it work. Just remember: You're still shoving a pillow through that opening, and there is only so much wiggle room.

Start by placing the two back pieces right sides together. Lay the zipper on the seam line in the center of the pillow and mark the zip stop at each end with chalk on the wrong side of the fabric. At the machine, stitch from the edge of the fabric to the first mark using a normal stitch; at the chalk mark where the zipper will begin, switch to your basting stitch; at the other chalk mark, where the zipper ends, switch back to your normal stitch. This allows you to rip out the stitches over the zipper without weakening the whole seam.

Follow the steps on the previous pages for installing the zipper, and when you get to using the tape to indicate the stitch line around the zipper on the right side, simply pivot at each end and create a box to surround the zipper. Easy!

147

Putting It All Together

With the zipper installed in the back of your pillow, your front and back should be the same size. Now it's time to put it all together!

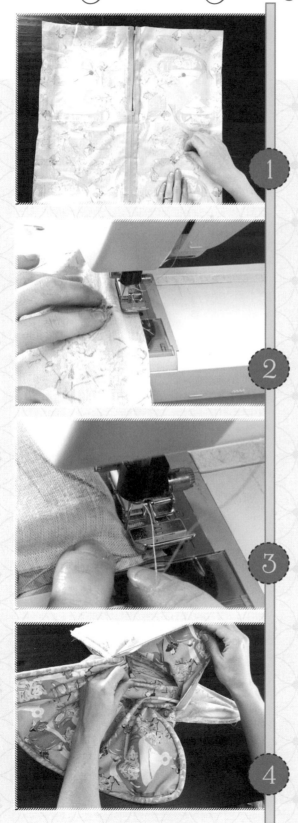

1. PIN BACK AND FRONT TOGETHER

Place the pillow front right side up on your work surface. Lay the pillow back, with the zipper partially unzipped, right side down on top of the front. Pin in place if you like, but you don't really need to. Add some pins in the center of the pillow to prevent shifting and bunching.

2. STITCH FRONT AND BACK

Using your zipper foot and regular stitch length, stitch all the way around the edges, keeping your stitches as close to the piping as possible. At the top and bottom edges, be sure to stitch through your zipper tapes to secure them.

3. PIVOT AT CORNERS

At the corners, stitch beyond the piped edge and then pivot with the needle in the fabric.

4. TURN PILLOW RIGHT SIDE OUT

Clip your corners at an angle before turning the pillow right side out. Then reach through the open zipper, grab the fabric of the front of the pillow and pull it right side out. Insert your pillow form, zip shut and you're done!

FOR MORE INSPIRATION

Pillows are one of the most asked-about projects, partly because store-bought ones can be so ridiculously expensive, but we all love the pop of color and warmth a pillow can provide. You've just made a nifty piped one with a zipper opening, but there are plenty of other styles to choose from. Some pretty examples are below.

Envelope closure (left) has an overlap at the back for easy swapping of covers; button loop closure (right) uses the buttons that hold the pillow inside as a design element.

Faux flange has the look of a more complicated pillow but is created by simple channel stitching.

Note: This project is designed to make two café curtain panels measuring 25" × 21" (64cm × 53cm) with a drop of 2¼" (6cm) from the rod. For narrower or wider, longer or shorter panels, simply adjust the width of the patchwork rows you include and the size of the lining.

PATCHWORK CAFÉ CURTAINS
WITH TAB-TOP PANELS

I didn't begin sewing as a quilter and usually think of myself as an apparel sewer. Having said that, I am constantly awed by some of the truly artistic creations that come from the quilting world. I've also been really excited to find so much history and connection in patchwork that I never knew was there. For example, despite the fact that I was the seventh member of my family to graduate from college in Florida, I never knew that Florida's Seminole American Indian tribe has its own unique style of patchwork or that such a thing could be so amazingly cool. This project is an adaptation of Seminole patchwork techniques and gives me a sense of continuity as I work. I hope you'll find it inspiring and that it will awaken a desire in you to see how far back into history sewing can take you.

shopping list + supplies

Basic Sewing Tools
(see page 23)

1 yard (91cm) each of five prints for the zigzag center panels

2 yards (1.8m) of an additional print (1 yard [91cm] will be the sixth print in the zigzag center panels, and 1 yard [91cm] will be for the coordinating side pieces and tabs)

1 yard of (91cm) fabric in a lighter color for curtain lining (bleached or unbleached muslin would work well, too)

matching thread

acrylic ruler

rotary cutter and cutting mat (optional)

skills you'll build

patchwork

linings

curtain tabs

hemming

151

Patching the Zigzag

This is the real show piece of the curtains: There are lots of café curtains out there, but the illusion of zigzagging lightning created by the patchwork is really stunning and unique. Add in all the colors and patterns available in quilting cottons today, and the possibilities are staggering.

1. CUT STRIPS FOR BLOCKS

Begin by cutting the strips. You'll need 14 strips for each curtain panel, so 28 strips total (for both). First, cut the two yards (1.8m) of side piece fabric apart to make two half-yards (46cm) and a whole yard (91cm). Set the whole yard aside. Place one of the half-yards, folded right sides together with selvages touching, on a cutting mat. Then layer each of the five prints on top, one after another, each of them also folded right sides together with selvages touching. Place the other half-yard on the top of the pile. This gives you a pile of seven fabrics total, and the first and last are the same fabric.

Line up the edges as closely as you can, then trim to get an even edge. Using a rotary cutter and acrylic ruler, cut four 2½" (6cm) strips lengthwise through the pile of fabric. You should end up with four sets of seven strips. When you unfold the pieces of fabric, each strip should measure 2½" × 45" (6cm × 114cm).

If you'd like to work with shears you can. Consider marking the 2½" (6cm) widths on the fabric with marking chalk and then trim each print separately.

2. STITCH FIRST TWO STRIPS TOGETHER

Using a ½" (1.3cm) seam allowance, take the first two strips of one set and stitch them right sides together along the long (45" [114cm]) edge. Keep in mind that the first and last strips should be the same fabric (the same as the side pieces you'll make later).

3. STITCH REST OF STRIPS AND BLOCKS

Stitch the remaining five strips in the same way, with their long edges together to create one large patchwork "block" made of the seven strips.

Repeat steps 2 and 3 with the additional sets of (seven) strips to create three more blocks of strips that are sewn together. Make sure to stitch the strips in the same order as you did the first block—that's the key to making the zigzag effect work. Press the seam allowances to one side on all four blocks.

4. CUT TWO BLOCKS ON THE BIAS TO THE RIGHT

Set one of the four blocks on the cutting mat. Use a clear acrylic ruler to find the bias line of the fabric—most have a handy 45-degree indicator marked on them that you can align with the edge of your fabric to determine the bias line. Cut a series of 2½" (6cm) strips on the bias (diagonal) with the lower edge of the ruler angled at your left and the upper edge of the ruler at your right. Cut strips across the fabric as long as you can still get all seven prints in the strip. Once you're no longer able to cut a 2½" (6cm) wide strip with all seven prints in it, stop cutting and toss the leftover pieces.

Repeat to cut strips from one other block. Be sure to keep your sets of strips together to avoid confusion later, since the order will matter.

(This step is a breeze using a rotary cutter, but shears do a great job, too. Simply chalk the cutting lines first, then cut the strips.)

5. CUT TWO BLOCKS ON THE BIAS TO THE LEFT

Repeat step 4 with the third and fourth blocks, but this time find the bias line running the opposite direction: with the lower edge of your ruler angled at your right and the upper edge angled at your left. This allows you to cut strips with opposite diagonals to create the zigzag effect in step 6.

6. LAY STRIPS TO CREATE ZIGZAG

Now you'll lay out the zigzag pattern for one curtain panel. Grab the strips from one block cut on the bias to the right (block 1) and one cut on the bias to the left (block 3). Place the strips next to each other, alternating a strip from block 1 with a strip from block 3. When you get enough strips placed, you'll see the zigzag pattern emerge. (Cool, huh?) When you're finished, you should have fourteen strips.

7. MATCH SEAMS

Place the first two strips with the right sides together along the long edges, making sure the seams of the strips match up (otherwise your zigzags won't look quite right). Stitch the strips together using a ½" (1.3cm) seam allowance.

8. STITCH STRIPS TOGETHER

Stitch each remaining strip to the one before it. Take care not to stretch the strips as you work, and watch to be sure that the seams match up as you stitch.

Repeat steps 6–8 with blocks 2 and 4 to make a second zigzag panel.

9. PRESS OPEN SEAM ALLOWANCES

When all the seams are stitched on both panels, press the seam allowances open on the back of the panels.

Finishing the Panels

To square off the edges and finish up the curtain panels, you'll add side pieces to each patchwork panel.

1. TRIM OFF EDGES

Trim off the triangles on the left and right (long) sides of each panel. This will creating new panels that measure about 17" × 21" (43cm × 53cm).

2. CUT AND PIN SIDE PIECES

Cut four pieces of the yard of fabric (which matches the top and bottom strips) measuring 4¾" × 21½" (12cm × 55cm). These will be the two side pieces for each curtain panel.

Lay out the central patchwork panel and then place one side piece along a side edge, right sides together. Pin in place. Repeat with the other piece on the other side of the panel.

Repeat to attach the side pieces to the second panel.

3. SEW ON SIDE PIECES

Stitch the side pieces to the patchwork panels using a ½" (1.3cm) seam allowance. It's best to place the fabric in the machine with the patchwork panel on top so you can ensure your seam allowances stay open as you stitch.

Making the Tabs

The tabs are basically a series of tubes pressed flat. In essence, this is the exact same thing you did for the handles on the tote bag (see page 114) and the ties on the sleep mask (see page 123), but on a larger scale.

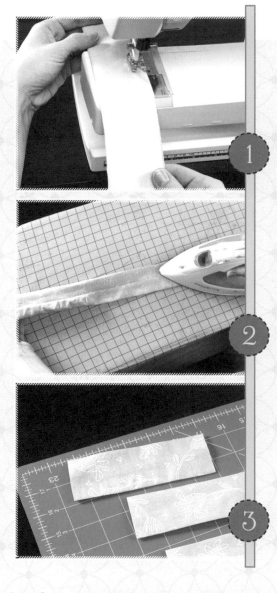

1. CUT, FOLD AND SEW TUBES

Cut four strips of fabric that measure 4½" (11cm) wide across the length of the fabric. (This fabric should match the side pieces on the panels.) I use my rotary cutter to create long, straight strips like this, because it's sure to make a straight cut, but you can use your shears, too.

Fold each strip in half lengthwise, and stitch along the long edge using a ½" (1.3cm) seam allowance.

2. TURN AND PRESS TUBES

Turn the tubes right side out. Then press the tubes with the seam at the center back. Work to get a good consistency in width along the whole tube to ensure that each of your tabs is equal in size.

3. CUT TUBES

Lay each tube out on your cutting surface. Measure 5½" (14cm) and cut; then repeat to the end of the strip. When you're finished cutting each tube, you should have fourteen tabs (all from one fat quarter!), enough for two curtains.

Stitch Tip

Making one long tube and then cutting it into smaller pieces is a great way to make a bunch of identical tabs or loops for any project. The best example of using this is in making belt loops. They're each meant to be the same size, but imagine how tedious it would be to stitch each one individually! Instead, make one looooong belt loop and then chop it up into the size you need.

Lining the Curtains

Because these curtains are made of patchwork, there are a lot of exposed seams on the back side. You want to cover those up so the view from outside the window is (nearly) as pretty as the one from inside. You can line the whole thing, nice and neat, to achieve that.

1. PIN ON TABS

Fold each tab in half with the center seam on the inside. With the right sides together and raw edges lined up, place seven tabs at the upper edge of the curtain panel. Start with the two end tabs, which should be ¾" (2cm) from the raw edges of the curtain panel. Space the remainder evenly along the upper edge. (By the way, an expandable seam measure is great in cases like this.) Repeat to pin the tabs to the other curtain panel.

2. LAY LINING OVER TABS

Cut two pieces of lining fabric 26" × 22" (66cm × 56cm). You'll want to catch the tabs between the lining and the curtain panel, in much the same way you caught the tote bag handles between the outer fabric and the lining on that project. So, with the curtain panel right side up and the tabs on top of it, lay the lining right side down over the tabs. Pin the lining in place. Repeat with the other curtain panel.

3. STITCH LINING AT TOP EDGE

Stitch along the upper edge of the curtain using a ½" (1.3cm) seam allowance, catching all the layers as you go (lining, tabs and patchwork panel).

4. STITCH LINING AT SIDES

Stitch the lining to the panel along the right and left sides using a ½" (1.3cm) seam allowance. Clip the upper corners. Leave the bottom 4" (10cm) of each side seam unstitched, so you can hem the curtain later.

Repeat steps 3–4 with the other curtain panel.

5. PRESS SEAMS

Turn the panels right side out. Press the seams on both panels, making sure each of the tabs is free and of equal length with its neighbors.

6. FOLD SIDES OF CURTAINS

On the sides of the curtain, fold the lower part of the curtain (the 4" [10cm] after the seam ends) to the inside 1½" (1.3cm) and press.

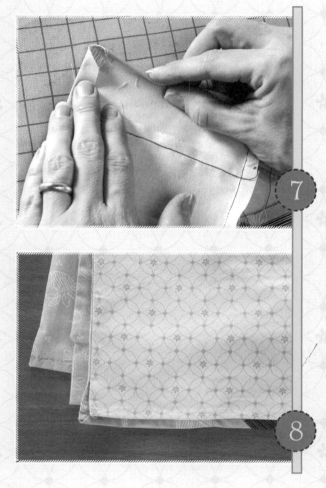

7. MITER CORNERS AND STITCH

At the lower edge of the patchwork panel, miter each corner by folding under ½" (1.3cm) and again ½" (1.3cm), and press in place. Stitch along the lower edge close to the fold.

If you'd prefer a hemless look, consider hand-stitching the hem on the zigzag panel in place for a clean finish.

8. STITCH LINING

Trim the lining, if necessary, so it lies even with the hem of the patchwork panel. Turn under ¼" (6mm) and then again another ¼" (6mm) to form a narrow hem. Stitch close to the edge. The lining should now be ½" (1.3cm) shorter than the patchwork panel. Tuck the last few inches of the lining under the side seams at the edge of the curtain panel. Complete the line of stitching you began there, leaving the lower hem free.

POWER PHRASE #3

66 THANKS! IT TURNED 99 OUT REALLY WELL

When you finish a project you've sewed from scratch, there is always a very strong temptation to apologize for the flaws. Say you've just whipped up a cute skirt and someone says, "Cute skirt!" Don't reply to that compliment by saying, "Yeah, but the hem is uneven, and the pocket didn't turn out the way I wanted …" Heck, no! Always say, "Thanks! It turned out really well." Plus, it prompts them to say, "Did you make that?" To which you can reply, "Yes. Yes, I did."

GIRL'S CHARM PACK SKIRT
WITH ELASTIC WAISTBAND

XXXXXXXXXXXXXXXXXXXXXXXXXXXXXXXXXXXXXXXXXXXX

Did you think way back at the first project that you'd even get this far? I gotta say, I'm super proud of you. You've mastered a serious mess of skills, and you've got a ton of cute projects to show for it.

And now? Now you're thinking clothes. Right on. I have a lot of students come through my classes for whom the idea of stitching clothing seems so far beyond their reach that they name it as their fantasy project, the one they'd stitch if time and ability were no object. I say, if you can stitch a straight line and a curve, you can totally tackle clothing.

This project is designed to ease you into clothing and build your confidence before releasing you into the wide world of apparel patterns (just a few pages away!). You'll be using precut fabrics, which means you can start sewing without having to worry about cutting perfectly right out of the gate. We'll cover some foundational skills for working on clothing, and then you'll have the confidence to move on to garments! that are more complicated (and more fun).

shopping list + supplies

Basic Sewing Tools
(see page 23)

2–3 fabric charm packs
of 42 5" × 5" (13cm ×
13cm) squares or 84–166
5" × 5" (13cm × 13cm)
squares (depending on
size; see next page)

matching thread

1 yard (91cm) of woven
nonroll elastic, ¾" (2cm)
width

large safety pin

skills you'll build

patchwork

gathers

casings and elastic

hemming

matching side seams

Stitching the Rows

We're working with 5" × 5" (13cm × 13cm) squares, usually referred to as charm packs. These are precut packages of fabric that are often available from manufacturers or from independent fabric dealers. Because you know the exact dimensions of each piece of fabric, laying out the skirt is really just a matter of simple math. Below I give the number of squares required for a girl's size 3 skirt, with sizes 4, 5 and 6 in parentheses after each number. If you'd like to make a larger or smaller skirt, adjust accordingly.

1. MIX AND MATCH SQUARES

Lay out the squares in four rows using the number of squares appropriate for the size you're making: Row 1: five squares (6; 6; 7); Row 2: eight squares (9; 10; 11); Row 3: twelve squares (13; 14; 14); Row 4: sixteen squares (16; 17; 17). Mix and match the prints to create a pleasing composition. This will make the front of the skirt. Repeat for the back of the skirt.

Seam allowances on most clothing patterns are a standard ⅝" (1.6cm)—a frighteningly and annoyingly enormous measurement, if you ask me. On this project, because we're working with a pattern based on layout rather than cutting out, you'll reduce your seam allowance to ¼" (6mm) on all the minor seams and ½" (1.3cm) on the side seams.

2. STITCH SQUARES TOGETHER

Stitch each square in the first row to its neighbor using ¼" (6mm) seams, working your way across the row until until each square is stitched to the next. Repeat for the other rows on the front and the back of the skirt.

After all the rows are stitched, lay them out like you'll be putting them together, with the shortest rows above the longer ones. At this point, you can swap rows (of the same length) from the front to the back if you feel that too many of the same colors or patterns have fallen near one another.

Gathering

Now it's time to start putting all of these rows together to make the skirt front and back. You'll be gathering the upper edge of all but the top row to make each row the same length as the row above it. Gathering is a simple technique of manipulating fabric that allows you to give fullness and softness with minimal effort. There are a few different techniques for gathering, the most basic of which I'll teach you in the steps below. See the sidebar on page 165 to learn two other gathering techniques.

1. RUN GATHERING STITCHES IN ROW 2

Running gathers is a lot like basting: These are temporary stitches that serve to hold the fabric in place until you stitch it down permanently.

Set your machine to the longest straight stitch. Run a row of stitches along the long end of Row 2 ¼" (6mm) from the edge. Run a second row at ⅜" (1cm) from the edge. Leave long tails of thread coming from the end of the stitching.

2. PULL TO CREATE GATHERS

To create your gathers, hold the two gathering threads in one hand and pull back on the seams with your other hand. Move the fabric smoothly along the gathering thread as you work, taking care not to yank so hard that you break your thread.

Stitch Tip

Make sure your gathering stitches are not too far above or below the seam line. If they are, your seam stitches tend to press them over on one another, making itty-bitty pleats as opposed to smooshing them into a flattened U shape. (Ultimately, this is the difference between a pleat and a gather: One is a fold that is pressed to one side [the pleat], and one is a loop that has been stitched flat [the gather].) By putting your gathering stitches directly on the seam line, you make it possible to achieve the greatest fullness you can.

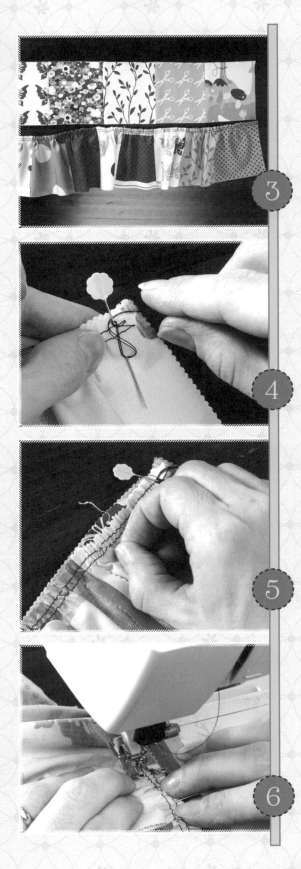

3. FINISH GATHERING AND PIN

Continue gathering until the upper edge of Row 2 is equal in length to the lower edge of Row 1. Then set the two rows right sides together and pin in place at each end.

4. WIND THREAD AROUND PIN

Wind your gathering thread around the pins at each end of the row; this keeps the threads in place for the next step.

5. MAKE GATHERS EVEN AND PIN

It's always worth your time to adjust your gathers and even them out as much as possible. With the pins in place, you can move the gathers freely along the stitches knowing they won't fall off at the ends.

After you've evenly adjusted your gathers, pin along the length of the edge to secure the two rows to one another prior to stitching the seams that join them.

6. STITCH ROWS 1 AND 2 TOGETHER

Set the machine to the regular stitch length. Stitch Row 1 and Row 2 together, right on top of your gathering line (⅜" [1cm]), between the two seams. Take care to keep as much roundness in the gathers as you can.

7. REPEAT WITH OTHER ROWS

Repeat steps 1–6 for the remaining rows on the skirt front until each row is gathered and stitched to the one above it. When you're finished stitching, press all seam allowances toward the top of the skirt.

8. SEW FRONT AND BACK SIDE SEAMS

Repeat steps 1–7 to make the back of the skirt. Then place the front and back right sides together, making sure to match the side seams in the rows. Sew both sides together using a ½" (1.3cm) seam allowance.

Alternate Methods for Gathering

As I mentioned, you have options when it comes to creating gathers. If you choose to use one of the gathering methods below, you still create the gathers along the seam line.

Method #1: Zigzag stitch over cording

In this method, you to move the fabric along a "rod." Lay a piece of thin cording down on the seam line. Zigzag stitch over the cording. Remove the skirt from the machine and then slide the fabric along the cord to create gathers. Pull the cording all the way out of the seam once the gathers have been stitched in place.

Method 1

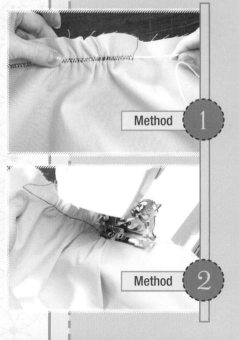

Method #2: Ruffler attachment

Some machines have a ruffler attachment that will create gathers for you. Attach the ruffler foot to the machine arm, and set the depth of the gathers you'd like to create. Then place the fabric under the foot and off you go! You will probably have the most success if you do a test run first.

Method 2

Creating the Elastic Waistband

A casing is a channel through which you guide elastic or a drawstring to create a waistband. Creating a casing is an easy technique that can be used in about a million places, so it's a good skill to know.

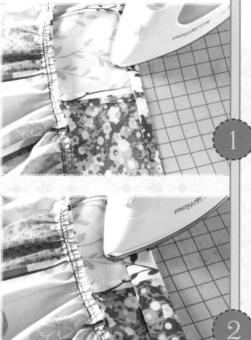

1. FOLD OVER EDGE

To start the casing, fold over the upper edge of the skirt about ¼"(6mm). Press that in place.

2. FOLD EDGE AGAIN

Then fold the upper edge over again, making a casing the right size for the elastic you'll add, and press. For this project, you're using ¾" (2cm) elastic, so fold over just a teensy bit more than ¾" (2cm) to give the elastic some wiggle room.

At-a-Glance Guide to Elastic Widths

Things like elastic, which seem so simple, can often be confusing when you're at the store and confronted with a whole world of products and no idea how to select the right one for your project. The widths available for elastic in the shops vary, and different widths are best suited to different tasks. Here's a quickie guide to help you sort them out.

¼" (6mm): best for sheet corners, baby clothing and sleeves but won't stand up to use in a waistband

⅜" (1cm): often called for at cuffs

½" (1.3cm): generally best when used for crafts and bags or pillows

¾" (2cm) and **1"** (3cm): make great waistbands because of their size and strength

3. STITCH CASING, LEAVING AN OPENING

Stitch the casing in place starting at the center back. Stitch very close to the folded edge to make sure the whole casing is stitched down.

When you get almost back to where you started stitching, leave an opening where you'll insert your elastic. It doesn't need to be huge, just about 1½ fingers wide. Be sure to backtack on either end of this opening because you'll want it strong enough to withstand running elastic through it later.

4. INSERT ELASTIC IN CASING

Now put in the elastic. First, cut a length of elastic the same measurement as the child's waistline. (This gives you an extra inch for overlap when you stitch it closed, plus just the right amount of stretch without squeezing little tummies.) Then find the biggest safety pin you have. (Most times, I use a diaper pin, because it's large and won't easily get lost.) Pin the safety pin through the end of the elastic. Then place the safety pinned end into the opening you left when you stitched the casing.

5. ANCHOR OPPOSITE END

To prevent the other end of the elastic from being sucked into the casing, use a pin (or smaller safety pin) to anchor it outside of the casing.

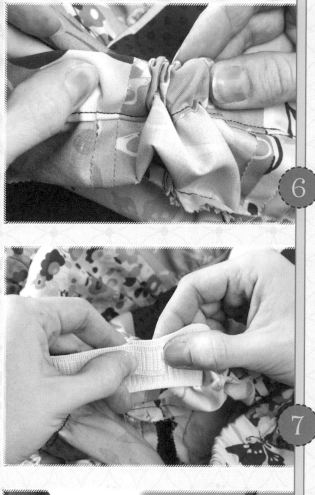

6. PULL ELASTIC THROUGH

Push the pin through the casing, and the elastic will follow behind. Push the safety pin along, allowing the casing fabric to bunch up as you go. After you've got a big ol' bubble of fabric bunched up behind the pin, slide the fabric over the elastic, holding the pin in place by pinching it through the fabric. Keep going all the way around the casing until the pin comes out the other side, dragging the elastic with it.

7. OVERLAP ENDS

Pull out about 3" (8cm) of elastic on either end. Overlap the ends by about 1" (3cm).

8. STITCH ENDS TO FORM LOOP

Stitch the two ends together on top of the overlap, going forward and backward about three to four times to get a good anchor going. You need this to be strong!

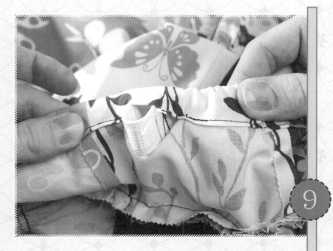

9. PUSH SECTION INSIDE CASING

Once the two ends are secure, you'll have a section of elastic outside the opening in the casing. Pull the section to the inside of the casing.

10. STITCH OPENING CLOSED

Stitch the small opening in the casing closed. Be sure to match the line of stitching around the rest of the casing for consistency.

11. STITCH ELASTIC TO SIDE SEAMS

Stitch through the elastic at the side seams to prevent it from shifting and rolling over. (I really, really hate it when the elastic gets all twisted inside the casing, mostly because it's really uncomfortable.) Stitch forward and backward through the elastic three to four times at each side seam.

Stretch the skirt out and evenly distribute the volume of the gathers on either side of the seams.

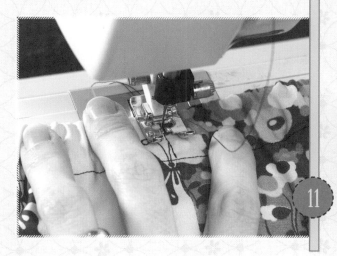

Hemming

Hemming a garment simply involves taking the lower edge and folding it to disguise the unfinished threads. There are two ways of doing this for your skirt: an overcast edge or a double-folded hem.

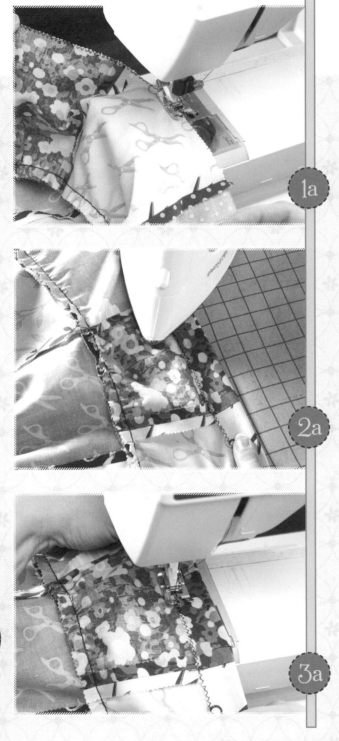

OPTION A: OVERCAST EDGE

The option is great if you'd like to shorten your work and have a quicker hem.

1. OVERCAST THE EDGE

Overcast the edge of the hem using a zigzag stitch like you did when you made your set of napkins (see pages 86–87).

2. FOLD OVER EDGE

Fold up the overcast edge 1" (3cm) and press it in place all the way around the hem. If you've pressed well, you might not need to pin the hem in place, but if you do, add your pins perpendicular to the cutting line spaced about 8"–9" (20cm–23cm) apart. You don't need to drown yourself in pins here; just add enough to ensure that your hem will remain at a consistent depth all the way around.

3. STITCH HEM

Stitch directly on top of your overcast edge to secure the hem in place. Remember to backtack at the end after you've sewn all the way around and your stitches run back over themselves.

1b

2b

OPTION B: DOUBLE FOLDING

If you'd prefer a slightly cleaner finish and are willing to spend a bit more time at the iron to achieve it, then this second hem technique is for you.

1. FOLD UNDER EDGE

Fold under the raw edge of the hem ¼" (6mm) and press it in place all the way around the skirt.

2. FOLD EDGE AGAIN AND STITCH

Fold the edge under another ¾" (2cm) and press it again. Then stitch, very close to the pressed edge.

You're done! How cute is that? I totally knew you could make clothes. So let's try something even cooler, shall we?

FOR MORE INSPIRATION

OK, I'm not usually into the matchy-matchy look, but sometimes it's pretty cool. Like here, for example. Larger squares of the same fabrics create a larger scale skirt for mom. Follow all the same steps as for the charm pack skirt, but replace the charm pack with a layer cake: 10" × 10" (25cm × 25cm) squares of fabric that are precut and pinked just like the charm pack squares are. Easy-peasy, matchy-matchy!

VARSITY LESSONS: SEWING CLOTHES

I truly and deeply adore making clothing. There is something so empowering about knowing that I can honestly make any garment I want, from skirts to blouses to dresses, even undies and shoes. I think a lot of it is the inherent potential in that knowledge—the ability to walk into a pattern shop and pick out anything, and then combine it with my favorite fabric du jour and make a one-of-a-kind reflection of who I am inside. The dreaming is part of the excitement, part of the appeal, like planning a road trip: The trip is fun, but the planning is where the dreams are.

If you're worried about whether your skills are up to the challenge, though, the dreaming is severely limited. I don't want you to look at a pattern and think, "Yeah, but I could never make this." Horse puckey! Sure you can. Following a pattern is just like anything else in sewing: The more you do it, the better you get at it. And unlike so many other areas in our lives, the more you work from a pattern (believe it or not), the more you might realize you don't need one at all! I know, it seems like a fantasy. So let's take small steps to get you there.

The three projects included in this chapter will require you to cut fabric from a pattern. (Yes, you've done a teeny bit of that in the last chapter, but this is some heavy-duty pattern stuff here.) Now, they're not printed on tissue like the ones you'd find in the fabric shop, and there's a reason for that (besides the fact that you'll need to print them yourself from the enclosed CD): The vast majority of preprinted patterns are multisize patterns. That means just what it sounds like—that there is more than one size on each pattern piece. That many lines all in one place can be confusing, especially if you've never cut and stitched from a pattern before. So you'll start with single-size patterns to give you the opportunity to work on perfecting those skills first, and then you'll move up to a multisize pattern for the final project. By the time you're done, you'll be ready to take on any pattern you come across. After that, the world! Fear not, young grasshopper: I believe in you. A journey of a thousand miles, after all, begins with a single stitch.

FIVE

USING COMMERCIAL PATTERNS

Reading the Pattern Envelope

Store-bought, commercial patterns come in envelopes that are loaded with information—and that most people ignore or overlook! A pattern envelope provides a chart (see example below) that gives you what you need to know: sizing information to help you select which size pattern to cut (and it's almost certainly not the size you buy off the rack); yardage so you'll know how much fabric to buy; a list of notions and supplies you'll need to complete the pattern and how much or many to buy of each; and measurements of the finished garment so you can anticipate how it will fit once you have it on.

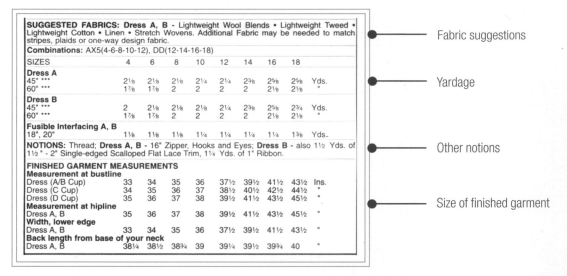

SUGGESTED FABRICS: Dress A, B - Lightweight Wool Blends • Lightweight Tweed • Lightweight Cotton • Linen • Stretch Wovens. Additional Fabric may be needed to match stripes, plaids or one-way design fabric.
Combinations: AX5(4-6-8-10-12), DD(12-14-16-18)

SIZES	4	6	8	10	12	14	16	18	
Dress A									
45" ***	2⅛	2⅛	2⅛	2¼	2¼	2⅜	2⅝	2⅝	Yds.
60" ***	1⅞	1⅞	2	2	2	2	2⅛	2⅛	"
Dress B									
45" ***	2	2⅛	2⅛	2⅛	2¼	2⅜	2⅝	2¾	Yds.
60" ***	1⅞	1⅞	2	2	2	2	2⅛	2⅛	"
Fusible Interfacing A, B									
18", 20"	1⅛	1⅛	1⅛	1¼	1¼	1¼	1¼	1⅜	Yds.

NOTIONS: Thread; **Dress A, B** - 16" Zipper, Hooks and Eyes; **Dress B** - also 1½ Yds. of 1½ " - 2" Single-edged Scalloped Flat Lace Trim, 1¼ Yds. of 1" Ribbon.

FINISHED GARMENT MEASUREMENTS

Measurement at bustline									
Dress (A/B Cup)	33	34	35	36	37½	39½	41½	43½	Ins.
Dress (C Cup)	34	35	36	37	38½	40½	42½	44½	"
Dress (D Cup)	35	36	37	38	39½	41½	43½	45½	"
Measurement at hipline									
Dress A, B	35	36	37	38	39½	41½	43½	45½	"
Width, lower edge									
Dress A, B	33	34	35	36	37½	39½	41½	43½	"
Back length from base of your neck									
Dress A, B	38¼	38½	38¾	39	39¼	39½	39¾	40	"

Fabric suggestions

Yardage

Other notions

Size of finished garment

Pattern Sizing

Were you a little concerned when I said that the size on the pattern envelope was almost certainly not the one you wear off the rack? It's true: Sewing pattern sizing is closer to classic couture sizing than to ready-to-wear sizing. We've all become lulled in recent years by the steady decrease in the size number that we wear as off-the-rack sizes have become bigger. So don't be shocked if you wear an 8 on the street but a 14 when you sew for yourself! It's just a reference point to help you select the correct pattern to fit *your* body. Part of the pleasure and privilege of stitching your own clothing is that you can make things to fit *you*. Don't let the number bog you down—you have a mission!

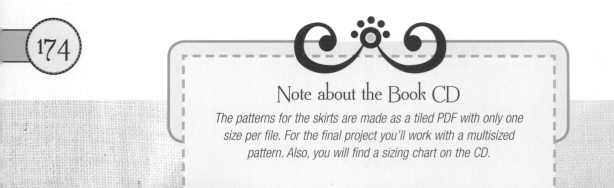

Note about the Book CD

The patterns for the skirts are made as a tiled PDF with only one size per file. For the final project you'll work with a multisized pattern. Also, you will find a sizing chart on the CD.

Preparing the Pattern: Iron That Bad Boy!

I can still remember the moment of possibly my biggest and most explosive sewing discovery: It was the dead of summer, and I was visiting one of my closest friends in Texas. We decided to stay up late in the night sewing, bonding, being silly. Now, this was early in my sewing career, when I often found that wrinkly pattern tissue combined with the wrinkly fabric made for edges that didn't line up and notches that never matched. My friend and I had a mutual brainstorm: Why not iron them both? First the fabric because that was kind of obvious. But then—the pattern itself! I know, crazy, right? But pattern tissue is plenty tough enough to stand up to the heat of your iron, and pressing it smooth allows you to get truly accurate cutting results when you lay it on your fabric.

Pattern Symbols

Patterns always tell you what you need to do. Every contemporary, commercially produced pattern is printed with text, cutting lines and a variety of symbols. Text on the patterns tell you what each piece is for and how many of each piece to cut. Lines and symbols indicate where pieces line up when putting fronts to backs, for example, or where to place buttons and buttonholes. Here's a breakdown of what each is and where it's most likely to be used.

Notch: These are used to indicate places where pattern pieces line up, which allows you to put the garment together easily. Single notches indicate the fronts of a garment, and double notches are used to indicate the garment back.

Circle: Circles are usually used to indicate where you ought to start and stop a particular technique, like gathering or placing pleats.

Grainline: This indicates how the pattern piece should be oriented in relation to the selvage. Place the grainline parallel to your selvage edge on the fabric. If you want to strive for perfection, you can place your ruler along the grainline indicator and the selvage.

Cut on fold: This means the pattern piece is designed to be cut on a folded piece of fabric that is then opened to a symmetrical shape. Place the edge of the pattern piece exactly on the fold, with no lumps or bumps that might throw off the measurements.

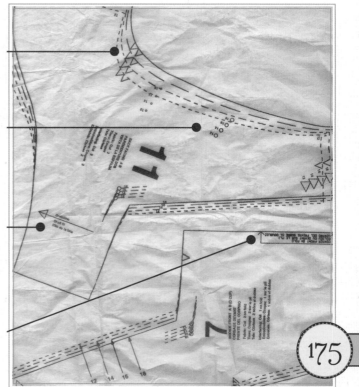

175

Pattern symbols should be transferred to your fabric on the wrong side. If you put them on the right side not only will you be marking up the side of your fabric that will be visible when your project is done, but you won't be able to see them as you're stitching, and that defeats the purpose.

Pinning Technique

When pinning the pattern to the fabric, keep in mind the goal is to distort the shape of the fabric as little as possible. Now, here's the thing: You don't really have to pin while cutting. Heretical? Anarchistic? Maybe. But totally true. There is a whole school of sewing that advocates no pins when cutting (or when stitching for that matter). Nutty, right? Despite that, here's my advice to newer stitchers: Pin for now. It gives you a more confidence and it allows you that moment to breathe and know everything is in the right place. And as you learn more and try new things, see if you want to *adios* those pins altogether. Some people don't and some do—and they're all good people. I just want you to be aware that sometimes the stuff you assume is most essential really isn't, and that you get to be the one to decide.

PROPER PINNING

When pinning the paper pattern to the fabric, place your pins parallel to the cutting line. Also pin in two places (see example below). Also, I recommend leaving the pins in even after you've cut the piece. This is useful if you have many pattern pieces to cut, or if you'll be setting the project aside for a bit and coming back to it later.

Proper pinning versus bad pinning
The photo on top shows the proper way to pin: parallel to the cutting line and pinned in two places. Putting the pin through twice holds the fabric and pattern firmly but gently, and helps keep everything where it ought to be as you cut. The photo below shows the wrong way to pin. The problem here is that the pin only goes into the fabric at one point, rather than two, and so won't actually hold anything in place. For pins to provide you with the confidence you crave, you really want them to anchor the fabric in place.

176

Stitch Tip

For 80% of patterns, when the pattern piece says "cut 2" you want to place the fabric right sides together in a double thickness to cut. However, there are situations when a pattern will indicate if you should cut a piece different than the standard—for example, when a particular pattern piece is too wide to fit on a 45" width of fabric. In those cases, follow the instructions printed on the pattern or included in the instructions. Also, pattern pieces are meant to all fit on one cut of fabric when possible to make the most efficient use of yardage. So when placing the pattern pieces on the fabric prior to pinning, arrange them until the pieces fit on a single cut of fabric.

As you place the pins through the pattern and into the fabric, most folks want to put their hand under the fabric and push the pins through. When you do this, it distorts the shape of the fabric, which is the absolute last thing you want to do! Remember, whatever shape the fabric has when you pin is the shape you'll be cutting out. Because you follow the cut edges of the fabric as you stitch, 90 percent of your results are determined when you cut. This might be time-consuming, but it's totally a good investment of your energy.

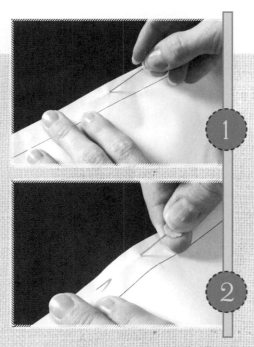

1. INSERT PIN
Use the cutting surface on which you've laid out the fabric to "reflect" the pins back to you as you put them through the fabric. Do this by placing your hand flat on top of the fabric, holding it steady against the table. Then take the pin in your hand and push the point into the fabric.

2. PUSH BACK THROUGH
When you hit the table, pull up ever so slightly on the pin until you're able to slide the point along the table and push it back up through the fabric.

Cutting

And now is the time in sewing when you actually cut! By now, you know that cutting is a critical step—taking your time here and really doing your best work will so completely pay off later you'll be glad you did. Use the proper cutting technique you already know to cut the pattern plus fabric the same way you would cut fabric alone (keeping the lower blade steady against the work surface). Be careful to cut the pattern and fabric the same size.

CUTTING NOTCHES
When cutting notches, you have two options: You may either cut a snip into the notch, right up to the point, which marks the fabric into the seam allowance; or you may cut outside the seam allowance in the shape of the notch. I prefer the latter because it's less likely to weaken the seam later, and there's less danger that I might cut too deeply and create a flaw where there wasn't one before.

177

CARPORT WRAP SKIRT
WITH ON-SEAM POCKETS

This design is based on a skirt I found in a friend-of-a-friend's carport when I was in college. I thought it was a huge piece of fabric draped over a butterfly chair and asked it I could take it home (that's me, always looking for free fabric!). When I lifted it to fold it up, I found that it was a wrap skirt in the cutest vintage print! A delightful surprise. I continued to wear the skirt for years until it quite literally fell off me from being worn out.

This pattern is an updated, more modern version of that vintage piece and features a sassy shorter length and a saucy button front.

shopping list + supplies

Basic Sewing Tools (see page 23)

pattern (printed and cut) for the Carport Wrap Skirt, found on book CD

2 yards (1.8m) of quilt- or dress-weight cotton, twill or denim (sizes 12 and 14 will require 2¾ yards (2.5m)

matching thread

fusible interfacing

buttonhole foot

marking chalk

seam ripper (optional)

two buttons

skills you'll build

reading a pattern

cutting technique

pinning technique

stitching seams

on-seam pockets

hemming

adding ties

creating buttonholes

179

Prepping the Pieces

Putting the pattern down on the fabric is always a moment of excitement tinged with caution for me—I want to be sure to get it right the first time. Diving in with wild abandon is totally great, and usually what has to happen. Hesitate, and you'll think and think and think and never cut anything out. Be brave here, review the tips on pinning and cutting patterns (on pages 176–177), and jump in!

1. PIN PATTERN TO FABRIC

Pin the pattern pieces to your fabric. Remember, the pattern will indicate how many of each piece you'll need and whether the pattern should be placed along a fold in the fabric. Follow the tips and techniques we discussed on the previous pages as you pin.

2. CUT FABRIC PIECES

Cut out the pieces, making sure to cut notches where noted in the pattern. For the pieces along the fold, just cut out the three sides and leave the fold uncut. (Note that on sizes 4–8, the two skirt fronts are cut together, in a double thickness. But for sizes 10–14, the two pieces are cut separately, on a single thickness.)

After your pieces are cut, separate the fronts and back. (Note that for this project, you cut three skirt pieces—two for the front and one for the back.) Lay out your pieces and make sure you have enough of each—check the pattern pieces to verify whether you were meant to cut one or two of each pattern piece and that all the fabric pieces are in order before moving on.

Stitch Tip

If you'd like, you can zigzag the edges of each piece prior to stitching them together, using the same technique we used on the napkins back in the very first project. This is an optional step, but really does make for a tidier finish when you're done (and when the project comes out of the wash).

Creating On-Seam Pockets

Pockets, if you ask me, are essential to the comfort and long-term love I have of wearing a skirt. I like all kinds of pockets, but some skirts demand that they be hidden, creating a secret place to stash your ID and lip balm. On-seam pockets do that by tucking into the side seam where you can use them, but they still remain out of view.

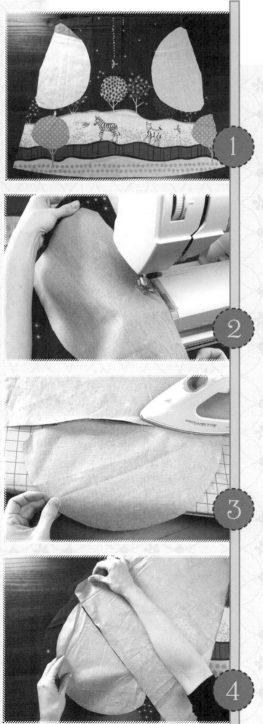

1. PLACE POCKET PIECES ON SKIRT FRONT

Place two of the pocket pieces on the back of the skirt at the side seams. Place the fabric with the right sides together, and be sure to line up the notches on the skirt with the notches on the pocket. Pin in place.

2. STITCH POCKETS TO SKIRT

Stitch the notched edges of the pockets to the skirt side seams using a ⅝" (1.6cm) seam allowance. The pieces should connect only at the seam line, not along the entire length of the pocket (in other words, where the edges match up).

3. PRESS SEAM ALLOWANCES

Press the seam allowances toward the pocket so the pocket faces away from the skirt.

Repeat steps 1–3 to attach the two remaining pocket pieces (one each) to the right skirt front and left skirt front.

4. PLACE FRONT AND BACK TOGETHER

Place the skirt front and skirt back with the right sides together, matching the pocket pieces and the seams. Because this skirt is a wrap, there is a left front piece and a right front piece. Place the right front piece right sides together with the skirt back, and lay them to overlap so you can access the seams. Repeat with the left skirt front. Alternately, you could stitch the side seam for the left and then go back and do the seam for the right. Just check your work to be sure you're not stitching the wrong edge.

5. SEW FRONT AND BACK TOGETHER

Stitch the skirt fronts to the back at the left and right side seams, matching notches and using a ⅝" (1.6cm) seam allowance leaving the side seams unsewn where the pockets have been stitched. Do not stitch straight down from top to bottom, or you will sew the pockets shut. Instead, stitch from the top down, then along the curve of the pocket, and pick up the side seam below the pocket, continuing the seam all the way to the bottom.

5

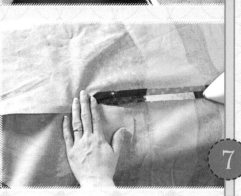

6. SNIP SEAM ALLOWANCES

Snip the seam allowance on the skirt below and above the pockets. This allows the seam allowances to open out properly. Also clip the curves on the pocket edges. This will let your pockets lie smoothly under the skirt.

6

7. PRESS SEAM ALLOWANCES

Press your seam allowances open to the base of the pockets, and press the seam allowances above them toward the pocket.

7

POWER PHRASE # 4

66 DOES IT BOTHER ME ENOUGH? 99

There is a place for attention to detail and perfect results in any endeavor. There is also a place to allow for imperfections and the added personal touch they provide. Handmade things often have teeny idiosyncrasies that make them all the more valuable to us—and your projects are handmade! Rather than beat yourself up over every little bobble or misstep, ask yourself: Does this imperfection bother me enough? Enough to tear it out and do it over? Enough to take the time to restitch this seam or remove and reinstall this zipper? Maybe this isn't a prototype, and you're planning to give the finished project as a gift. Or maybe this is a quickie little something for the kids. Or maybe you're tackling a tough vintage pattern and making an investment piece with really fabulous (expensive) fabric. Your answer to the question, "Does it bother me enough?" might be different in each case. Just keep reminding yourself that perfection is relative to the project, and although you might strive for it in some things, it's not essential in every piece of sewing you touch in order to consider yourself skilled and knowledgeable. You're so hard core at this point, and you don't even know it—keep it in perspective, yo, and don't let it go to your head!

Stitching the Button Loops and Front Band

For this skirt, you'll make some sassy button loops for closures at the front. One of the things I disliked about the original college-era design was the tendency it had in high winds to flip open and reveal a little more than I liked of my leg. Let's solve that problem here by adding some modesty buttons that also serve to up the style factor.

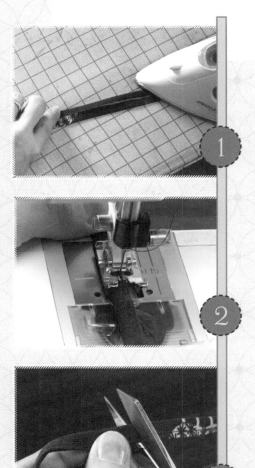

1. CUT AND PRESS STRIP FOR BUTTON LOOP

Cut a strip of fabric 8" × 1½" (20cm × 4cm) to construct the loops. Press in both long edges (about ⅜" [1cm]) so they meet in the middle. Then fold the strip in half lengthwise and press it nice and flat.

2. STITCH STRIP CLOSED

At your machine, stitch along one long edge of the button loop strip, close to the folded edges. The goal is to create a long, skinny tube that has been stitched closed along one long edge.

3. CUT STRIP IN HALF

Cut the strip in half to create two sections, each 4" (10cm) long. Each of these sections will become one button loop.

4. PIN LOOPS TO SKIRT

Fold each strip in half to create a loop. Place each button loop on one of the two dots on the left front side (on the outside) of your skirt. (Or space them apart as you see fit—it's your skirt, after all!) Pin each button loop in place with the pin horizontal to the skirt edge (so you can stitch over it when you put everything together).

5. PRESS EDGES OF FRONT BANDS

Press in one long edge of each front band piece, about ³/₈" (1cm). (You'll attach these when you attach the button loops on the previous page).

6. STITCH FRONT BANDS TO SKIRT

Take one of the front band pieces and place it right sides together with the unsewn vertical edge of the left skirt front, sandwiching the button loops between the two and lining up all raw edges. Pin in place, if you like. Stitch all layers together using a ⁵/₈" (1.6cm) seam allowance, running through the ends of the button loops as you go.

With the right skirt front, take the remaining front band and lay the two right sides together with raw edges lining up. Stitch together using a ⁵/₈" (1.6cm) seam allowance.

7. GUTTER STITCH FRONT BANDS

Remember when you gutter stitched the place mat in the last chapter? Here's another place you can use that skill: attaching the front bands. If you choose not to gutter stitch here, you can also topstitch close to the seam line to catch the underside of the front band in place.

Mitering the Hem

This skirt is kicky and light, and perfect for wearing on a breezy day at the park. Because it's a wrap front, you want the hem and finishing to be pretty, too, because there's a good chance it'll get seen once in a while. Let's miter the hem and tuck it all away so it's something to be proud of.

1. FOLD OVER CORNER AND HEM

Start with the corners at the bottom front edges of the skirt. Using the same technique as the fancy napkin miter (see page 88), fold back the corner where the hem and front band meet to create a triangle. Press in the hem about ½" (1.3cm).

2. FOLD TO MITER CORNER

Fold in the front band and the hem again so they meet at the corner, creating a nice mitered point.

3. STITCH CORNER

Stitch close to the folded edge, pivoting at the corner, along the lower edge. Ideally, the stitches you put in for your hem will begin and end at the line of stitches you used to topstitch the front band in place, creating the illusion of a single line of stitching.

Adding the Waistband & Ties

The waistband for this skirt is a simple one. You'll apply fusible interfacing to the waistband before stitching it on. As you learned in the belt project (see page 130), interfacing is used to give weight and sturdiness to projects. In the belt project, you used sew-in interfacing and slipped the interfacing inside the belt. But for this project, you'll use attach fusible interfacing to the waistband.

Interfacing: Choosing and Using It

Interfacing comes in different weights. The rule of thumb is for the interfacing to be lighter than the fabric you plan to use it on, so it won't overwhelm the project. Interfacing is available as fusible or sew-in, and either can be used in most projects. Fusible interfacing bonds permanently to the fabric when pressed under the iron. Some folks really don't like fusibles, mostly because of the glue factor. For me, in most circumstances, I prefer fusible, mostly because it's quick and easy. Sew-in interfacing can be either a purchased product or can be another fabric, like flannel or silk, that gives body to your garment. It works great, especially for handbags and really detailed projects. I use sew-in when I'm making an investment piece but not when I do everyday sewing.

1. PRESS INTERFACING TO WAISTBAND PIECES

Cut two pieces of interfacing slightly larger than the waistband pieces that you've already cut out. Place a waistband piece right side down on the ironing board and lay the interfacing on top of it, fusible side down. On most brands, the fusible side feels slightly bumpy or textured to the touch; that's the heat-activated glue that you're feeling, and you want that on the wrong side of the fabric and not on the underside of your iron.

When using fusible interfacing, the heat setting is important. Make sure it's hot but not flaming, or it'll eat your interfacing. Then press—don't iron—the interfacing by moving the iron in overlapping arcs across the fabric. Repeat with the other waistband piece.

2. TRIM EXCESS

After the interfacing is cool and set, trim the excess edges to match up with the waistband pieces. From here on out, the interfacing-and-fabric combos are treated as one piece of fabric.

Stitch Tip

Fusible interfacing has no grainline, so if you have remnants, you're free to cobble them together to cover the pattern piece. It won't show through as long as you keep the edges from overlapping a lot.

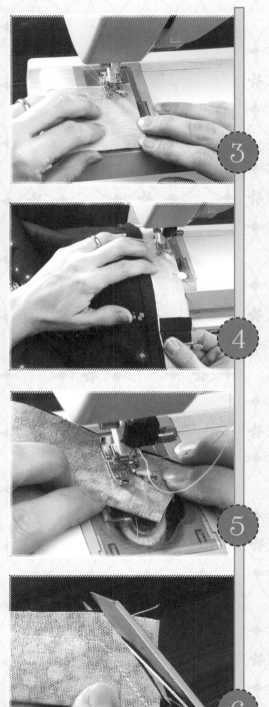

3. SEW WAISTBAND CENTER SEAM

Place the two waistband pieces right sides together and stitch a seam along one short end using a ⅝" (1.6cm) seam allowance. You should now have one long waistband piece with a seam at the center back. Fold over one long edge of the waistband about ⅝" (1.6cm) and press.

4. STITCH WAISTBAND TO SKIRT

Place the waistband against the upper edge of the skirt with the right sides together and the raw edges lined up, matching the waistband seam to the center back of the skirt. The folded edge should be toward the body of the skirt and away from the stitch line. Stitch along the edge using a ⅜" (1cm) seam allowance. Press the seam allowances toward the waistband.

5. FOLD AND STITCH TIES

Fold the two pieces for the ties lengthwise and right sides together. Stitch one piece with a ⅝" (1.6cm) seam allowance down the long edge. When you get to about 1" (3cm) from the end of the tie, pivot and stitch at the diagonal across to the corner. (This will create a pointed tie, rather than one with a squared-off edge.) Repeat with the other tie.

6. TRIM TIE AND TURN RIGHT OUT

Trim off the excess fabric at the point of each tie. Then turn the ties right side out, using the technique you used for the tote bag straps and the eye mask ties. Press the ties flat with the seam at the side.

7. PLEAT TIES TO FIT

Place the raw edge of one tie even with the raw edge of one side of the waistband. At the raw end of the tie, fold the tie to create a tiny pleat just big enough that the width of the tie is slightly less than half the width of the waistband (so it will fit inside the waistband when it's folded). Pin the tie in place to hold it while you repeat this step with the other tie on the other side of the waistband.

8. STITCH TIES IN PLACE

Fold the whole length of the waistband right sides together and sandwich the ends of both ties between the two layers of the waistband. Stitch both ties at a 5/8" (1.6cm) seam allowance north and south, parallel to the front opening of the skirt. This will leave the waistband unstitched along its folded, lower edge—that's correct for now.

9. PULL OUT TIES

Flip the waistband back over to the inside, hiding the ends of the ties and pulling the ties to the outside. Neat, huh? Now press along the upper edge of the waistband one more time to position it correctly before you stitch it down. Pin if you'd like. (By the way, you can even make a quick, easy apron using this same techique!)

10. STITCH WAISTBAND IN PLACE

Stitch the waistband in place along the edge that meets the skirt, either by stitching the ditch or by topstitching. Be sure to catch the entire lower edge of the waistband along the inside of the skirt.

Stitch Tip

If you want to have wide, fat ties for a skirt (like in the inspiration project on the next page), follow the same steps, just use a deeper pleat at the waistband.

Finishing Touches

These last few bits are the ones that many of us would like to avoid—I mean, you're so close to being done! But really, it's the little details that set your handmade garments apart and make them special, so make this last mile a good one!

1. CREATE BUTTONHOLE FOR TIE

Wrap the skirt around your waist to determine where the right-side tie will pass through the skirt from the inside to the outside on the left side. Mark the spot with chalk. At your machine, stitch a buttonhole about ¾" (2cm) in length (or a length to accommodate your buttons). (See pages 133–135 for a buttonhole refresher.)

2. SEW ON BUTTONS

Lay the skirt out flat and position the waistband as you will to wear the skirt (you can also put the skirt on yourself or on a dress form). Note where the button loops fall and mark a dot in chalk for the buttons. Sew the buttons in place, and sashay on out in your amazing skirt! (See page 137 for a button refresher.)

FOR MORE INSPIRATION

Feeling flirty and fun? Craft a romantic version of the classic wrap skirt from linen/Tencel blend. Use fatter ties, three rows of ruffles at the hem and cute little patch pockets to give the skirt character.

A-LINE SKIRT
WITH PATCH POCKETS

Putting your machine through its paces has given you some skills—more than I think you realize. Now you're ready for the big time: a skirt with an invisible zipper, adorable patch pockets and a fancy hem. For many stitchers, this is a kind of a Holy Grail; it's a truly wearable piece that goes with everything, is easy to sew, fits like a dream and makes you feel like a million bucks. The classic A-line skirt will never go out of fashion, it flatters every figure and will scream "boutique chic" everywhere you go. Remember, this project is another chance for you to learn techniques that you can use again and again, while creating a project you'll love to wear and show off—all while practicing your power phrase, "Thanks! It turned out really well."

shopping list + supplies

Basic Sewing Tools (see page 23)

pattern (printed and cut) for the A-line Skirt, found on book CD

2 yards (1.8m) of quilt- or dress-weight cotton, cotton twill or denim (you can use contrasting fabric for the waistband and hem facings, if desired)

fusible interfacing

7" (18cm) invisible zipper in coordinating color

matching thread

hem guide or seam gauge

blind hem stitch foot

zipper foot

skills you'll build

yokes and facings

invisible zippers

hems and hem facings

patch pockets

hand finishing inside garments

191

Prepping the Waistband and Skirt

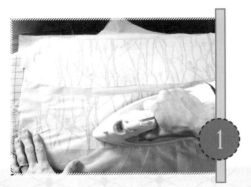

Some waistbands are just that: a skinny band at the waistline that attaches to the rest of the skirt. In this case, you'll be attaching a fatter waistband called a yoke: It has a shape of its own, adds some visual interest and allows greater support so you can adapt this pattern in infinite ways! We'll talk more about yoked waistbands in a few pages.

Stitch Tip

Most patterns ask you to cut out "1 of fabric, 1 of interfacing" for pieces that will be interfaced. The honest truth is that I don't do that. I find interfacing incredibly difficult to cut according to a pattern piece because it tends to slip all over the place. For most patterns, it's perfectly fine to fuse a larger piece of interfacing to the wrong side of the fabric and then trim it down to size.

Before you begin the yoked waistband, you'll need to cut out the yoke pieces along with all the other skirt pieces. Place your pattern pieces on the fabric and cut all the pieces out. Remember, the pattern will indicate how many of each piece you'll need and whether the pattern should be placed along a fold in the fabric. And check back on pages 174–177 for other tips!

1. FUSE INTERFACING TO WAISTBAND PIECES

Cut a piece of interfacing slightly larger than the two yoke front pieces. Press the interfacing to the pieces, on the wrong side of each.

At this point, you should have what looks like four identical pieces (unless you're using contrasting fabric for the facing), except two have interfacing fused to the wrong sides. These are the yoke front pieces (with interfacing), and the other pieces are for the yoke facing.

2. STITCH PIECES

With the right sides facing, stitch the waistband pieces together at the right side seam, matching the notches and using a ⅝" (1.6cm) seam allowance. Double check to be sure that this is your right (as you'll be wearing the skirt), since you'll want the zipper side to be on your left. Press the seam allowance open. Repeat this step with the yoke facings.

3. STITCH SKIRT FRONT AND BACK TOGETHER

With the right sides facing, stitch the skirt front and back together at the right side seam, using a ⅝" (1.6cm) allowance. The seam should be on the same side (of the finished skirt) as the yoke seam. Then press open the seam allowance.

Attaching the Patch Pockets and Waistband

Adding pockets is always easier when the garment is only partially finished, so it will lie flatter while you stitch them. For this skirt, you'll attach cute little patch pockets. Unlike the on-seam pockets that you added to the carport wrap skirt, which are hidden, patch pockets can be seen right on the front of the skirt, giving it a more casual look.

1. SEW POCKETS

You have two pieces for each pocket, so four pieces total. One is the pocket that will show to the public, and the other is the pocket lining. Stitch each pocket piece and pocket lining piece right sides together, leaving a small opening (to turn right side out later). Use a ½" (1.3cm) seam allowance. You should have two pockets.

On each pocket, trim the seam allowance to ¼" (6mm), and clip the corners and curves. Then turn the pockets right side out and press.

Stitch Tip

Remember: More clips in the seam allowance equals a flatter finish! If you're struggling to get a nice, crisp press, consider cutting teeny notches (like little pie pieces) rather than simply doing straight clips. This will remove more bulk, especially on thicker fabrics.

2. PIN POCKETS TO SKIRT

Pin the pockets in place on the skirt front. Placement is up to you, but a good rule of thumb is about 2" (5cm) from the top raw edge and 4" (10cm) from the side raw edges of the skirt front. Feel free to "try on" the skirt to check the placement. Also keep in mind that the yoke on this skirt drops about 4" (10cm) from your waistline, and take that into account.

3. SEW ON POCKETS

Sew the pockets to the skirt front. Stitch around three sides of the pocket close to the pressed edges. As you work your way around the lower edge of the pocket, catch the small opening (that you used to turn the pocket right side out) to close it up. Handy, one-step stitching!

4. STITCH WAISTBAND AND SKIRT TOGETHER

Before moving on, now's a good time to add the yoked waistband to the skirt. Pin the yoke (the piece with the interfacing) and skirt with the right sides together, matching the side seam and notches, and lining up the raw edges along the top of the skirt. Stitch the two together using a ⅝" (1.6cm) seam allowance. Then press the seam allowances toward the yoke.

193

Adding the Invisible Zipper

Can I tell you a secret? I like invisible zippers way better than the zipper you used on the pillow. But learning the invisible zipper first doesn't make it easy to learn the standard universal zipper, so that's why you began with the universal.

Invisible zippers are meant to be just that: invisible. There's a special foot for your machine that will install them (see the sidebar below), which is what I use. Having said that, for years and years, I installed these with my standard foot, so you will be fine using whatever you have. FYI, the invisible zipper is installed before you stitch any part of the left side seam, so no basting here!

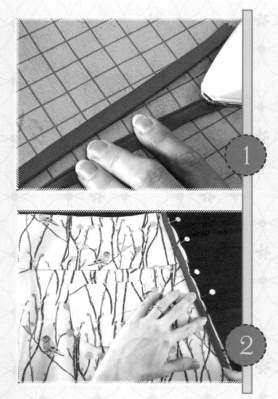

1. PRESS ZIPPER

Take a look at the front of the invisible zipper. Notice how you don't see the teeth? Now flip it over—there they are! The teeth are constructed here to roll to the back and pull the fabric of the seam with them, which is part of the invisibility magic. To get it all stitched together well, though, you want to open those teeth out and then stitch the fabric to the zipper tape. When the teeth roll back into place, the fabric will go with them.

Start by placing the zipper face down on the ironing board, unzipped. With the very tip of your iron, roll the teeth over so they are flat rather than curved. (They're plastic, but they won't melt—but don't hang out too long.) Press the zipper teeth open on the back of the zipper. This allows you to get super close to the teeth while you're stitching.

2. PIN ZIPPER TO SIDE OF SKIRT

On the open the left side of the skirt, pin the zipper with the teeth on the actual seam line—you'll be stitching the zipper tape, but the teeth themselves are the seam line for the rest of the seam, so we want those puppies right on the line of stitching. The teeth should be facing the center of the skirt not the raw edge. (This is opposite of how you'd expect to line things up, but it works out in the end.) I usually begin with the front of the skirt and then do the back, but it really doesn't matter where you begin.

The Invisible Zipper Foot: Why Buy?

Most machine models have a specialty foot available just for installing invisible zippers. It makes putting in these puppies really simple, and I recommend getting it (and you know I hardly ever tell you to run out and buy something). But it isn't essential. If you're not sure whether to invest in a new tool, keep asking yourself: Does it save me enough time and trouble that the cost is worth it to me?

3. STITCH ZIPPER TO SKIRT

Replace the machine's standard presser foot with your zipper foot (or invisible zipper foot, if you're lucky enough to have one). Stitch super-duper close to the teeth all the way down the zipper, stopping when the tip of the zipper foot touches the zipper pull. (If you're using the invisible zipper foot, use the groove on the bottom to guide your stitches.)

4. REPEAT WITH OTHER ZIPPER TAPE

Now pin the other side of the zipper to the other side of the skirt. As before, the tape goes along the raw edge and the teeth face in toward the center. Be extra careful to ensure that the two zipper tapes line up just right. If the tops of the zipper tape aren't aligned, when the zipper is installed the seam will be crooked, and the skirt won't lie flat against the skin.

Stitch the tape to the skirt as you did in step 3. Then zip it shut.

5. STITCH REMAINDER OF SIDE SEAM

Now move the lower zipper tape out of the way and begin to stitch the remainder of the side seam. Start just above where the zipper stitches end, and then carry the seam down the rest of the side of the skirt. This is the toughest part of working with an invisible zipper: getting that seam line in just the right place in relation to the stitches along the edge of the zipper. If they're too far away, your zipper will appear puckered. Take your time and stick it out— you'll get there!

6. PRESS OPEN SEAM ALLOWANCE

Press open the seam allowance below the zipper. The remainder of the seam allowances lie along the zipper tapes now and will lie flat all by themselves. Aren't you proud of yourself?

Completing the Yoked Waistband

A waistband is usually a piece of fabric 2" (5cm) in width or less that encircles the waist, gives the skirt body something to attach to and provides structure and support for the rest of the garment. A yoke, on the other hand, is a wider piece of fabric that does all of the above and provides additional shape and visual interest to the piece. As you know, in this skirt, we're using a yoked waistband to allow for a nice, A-line shape that will flatter any figure and to give a little more support in the tummy area. After all, who wants to make a cute little skirt that you can't wear on your less-than-perfect days?

1. PRESS EDGE OF WAISTBAND FACING

Fold over the longer (which is the lower) edge of the yoke facing ⅝" (1.6cm). Press the fold. Remember, the yoke facing is the piece without the interfacing you stitched on page 192. (I'm using a yoke facing in contrasting fabric.)

2. STITCH FACING TO YOKE

Open up the zipper and place the yoke facing right sides together with the yoke of the skirt, lining up the raw edges. The facing should extend beyond the waistband by ⅝" (1.6cm) on either end of the zipper (where you'll fold it under later). Pin the facing in place. Then stitch the facing to the yoke all the way around the upper edge. (FYI, it'll be easier to see your starting and stopping points if you place the work so the facing is on the throat plate and the remainder of the skirt is on top.) When you're finished, press the seam allowance in the direction of the facing.

3. UNDERSTITCH FACING

Understitching is a technique that attaches the facing to the seam allowances to prevent it from rolling to the outside and marring the shape of the skirt. It sounds awkward and tricky, but it's actually simple to do and makes a huge difference in fit.

Lay the fabric on the throat plate with the facings wrong sides up to you (and the seam allowances underneath). Using a ⅝" (1.6cm) seam allowance, stitch all the way around the waistline, parallel to the seam, through the facing and seam allowances only—and not through the outer waistband fabric. Use your default stitch length and backtack at each end.

Because you've pressed the seam allowances away from the yoked waistband pieces and toward the facings, the stitches will show on the inside of the skirt, along the seam line on the facings, but not on the outside of the skirt, on the yoke itself. Neat, huh?

196

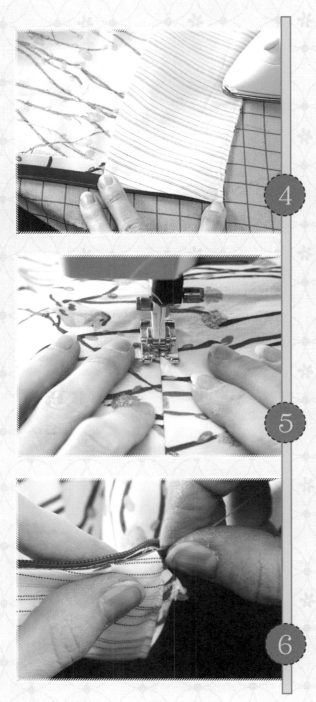

4. PRESS UPPER EDGE OF FACING AND SIDES

Flip the facing back to the inside of the skirt and press the upper seam flat. The lower folded edge should cover the stitches that attach the yoked waistband to the skirt.

Also fold under the facing's raw edges at the zipper, lining them up with the inside of the zipper teeth. Press the folds in place.

5. GUTTER STITCH

Place the skirt right side up on the machine. Gutter stitch the lower edge of the facing in place along the seam that attaches the yoked waistband to the skirt.

6. STITCH SIDE EDGES TO ZIPPER

Hand stitch the facing's folded side edges to the zipper tape using a slip stitch. (For a slip stitch refresher, see the eye mask on pages 126–127.)

Hemming the Skirt

Ease is that little extra amount of fabric that allows things to fit properly. Ease stitching uses thread to take up that extra fabric so that two pieces that don't fit flawlessly go together smoothly. To set up for the hem, you'll first do a double fold, using ease stitching to help it lay flat.

1. FOLD HEM

Turn the skirt wrong side out and fold up the lower edge (the hem) ½" (1.3cm) and press. (This is a great place to use a hem guide or seam gauge.) Then fold up another 1½" (4cm) and press in place (which is a total of 2" [5cm] for the hem). You'll notice that the folded edge doesn't quite lie flat against the rest of the skirt—that's because the A-line shape makes the circumference of the lower edge slightly larger around than the skirt above it, so they don't fit together perfectly. We're about to fix that.

2. RUN GATHERING STITCHES

Fold up the first (½" [1.3cm]) fold at the hem and stitch a row of gathering stitches near the edge of the hem. (See pages 163–165 for more on gathering stitches.) Then run another row of stitches just inside those, closer to the fold. (To make the next step easier, you might consider running multiple sets of gathering stitches [starts and stops] so you have a bunch of sections of gathering threads rather than one long one that goes all the way around.)

3. PULL UP EASE STITCHES

Fold up the second (1½" [4cm]) hem fold. Using the ease stitches, pull up on the ends of the thread and ever so slightly gather the fabric at the hemline, as shown. This will reduce the length of the edge at the hem. Do this all the way around the hem, taking care to make the hem match the circumference of the skirt above it and to adjust the gathers so they're even all the way around. (By the way, you won't have true gathers here. You should just have very slight puckers in the fabric.)

After the ease stitches have all been pulled up, use your iron's steam to relax those puckers and help your hemline lie flat.

To give a really professional look to this skirt, you'll use the blind hem stitch. The blind hem stitch works like this: The machine stitches straight for a bit just on the hem allowance, and then it jumps out and grabs the rest of the skirt and connects the two. On the outside, all that shows is the itty-bitty single stitch where the machine jumped out, and not all the long stitches, which are hidden in the hem allowance inside the skirt. It's pretty darn neat, but I strongly recommend doing some practice stitches with this technique first before working on your skirt.

4. FOLD FABRIC STITCH BLIND HEM

How the fabric is folded is the key to the blind hem stitch. Place your skirt wrong side up on your work surface with the hem folded up facing you. Then take the hem allowance and 2" (5cm) of skirt, and fold them back underneath the rest of the skirt so that just ½" (1.3cm) of the hem peaks out at you. The right sides of the skirt are touching one another, and the first fold you placed at the lower edge of the skirt (in step 1) is facing up at you.

Set your machine to the blind hem stitch. This is the one with the icon that looks like a heartbeat—long straight line, then a carrot, then more straight line. Replace the presser foot with the blind hem foot, if you have one. (If you're not using a blind hem foot, your standard foot for zigzag stitching will work fine, but take your time and really watch your work, because the regular foot won't keep the edges lined up for you the way the specialty foot will.)

Too create the stitch, begin with the hem allowance extended under the presser foot. You'll see that the needle jumps to the left every six or seven stitches—the goal is to line up the needle so that when the jump comes, it snags just a single thread of the fabric on the fold.

5. FINISHED!

In the finished project, you'll see where the straight stitches are on the hem allowance (invisible to the outside) and the carrot stitches are grabbing a single thread of the rest of the skirt, making nearly invisible indentations.

FOR MORE INSPIRATION

Adding a fancy scalloped hem can really make your work stand out. Here I've used a glass turned upside-down on the edge of the pattern hem to draw in scallops across the lower edge of the skirt. To do this, make a slight space between each arc, and then pivot your stitches as you come to that space. Cut one piece for each skirt panel, and another piece the depth of the scallops. Interface the scalloped fabric, then stitch right sides together with the skirt edge. Clip your curves, then turn to the inside and stitch in place. Voilà!

CAP-SLEEVED BLOUSE
WITH DARTS

XXXXXXXXXXXXXXXXXXXXXXXXXXXXXXXXXXXXXXXXXXXXXXXXXXXXXXXXXXXXXX

You've done so much so far! Do you realize that? This project is your graduation gift. It's not a final exam—more of a celebration of how all the skills you've been building really come together to create something beautiful that you can be truly proud of, something so cool that maybe you thought you wouldn't be able to do. I love it when I imagine something and then it actually comes to pass, and I really want that for you with this blouse. It has a little bit of everything: a dress shirt collar that's just a tiny bit oversized to keep it hip; a curved hem to emphasize your shape; darts front and back to pull in your waist; a breast pocket to mix some business with pleasure; sweet little cap sleeves for girlish charm; and a full button placket down the front. You'll look great in this—and best yet, the shape looks fantastic with both of your skirts.

So, jump in and have confidence: This is going to be fun!

shopping list + supplies

Basic Sewing Tools (see page 23)

pattern (printed and cut) for the Cap-Sleeved Blouse, found on book CD

2 yards (1.8m) of quilt- or blouse-weight cotton

matching thread

sew-in interfacing

marking chalk

acrylic ruler

buttonhole foot

knitting needle (or other turner)

seam ripper (optional)

6 fabric-covered button kits or 6 small buttons

skills you'll build

constructing collars and collar stands

bust and waist darts

curved hems

inset sleeves

facings

buttons and buttonholes

201

Making the Collar

Most blouse patterns have you begin with the shoulder seams, but I find more instant gratification out of constructing the collar first. Then I know I've really made something, and I'm motivated to keep sewing. This is a small piece that you can finish quickly and when you don't have a lot of time to devote to the project.

1

2

3

4

1. CUT OUT FABRIC PIECES

Lay your pattern pieces out on your fabric. Remember to place your fabric in a double thickness with the right sides together (unless otherwise noted) and transfer your markings. Cut out the fabric pieces. (Check back on pages 176–177 for pinning and cutting tips.)

You should now have two pieces of collar cut from the same pattern.

2. SEW INTERFACING TO COLLAR

Cut a piece of sew-in interfacing using the collar pattern. (Now, I know I said I prefer fusible interfacing, but for this project, we're using the sew-in method so you can learn how to do it and have that skill in your back pocket. After you've used both fusible and sew-in, you can better decide which method is best for you and your projects.)

Lay the interfacing on the wrong side of one collar piece. Baste the two together using a ⅝" (1.6cm) seam allowance. Press the collar piece nice and smooth.

3. TRIM INTERFACING

Trim outside the seam allowance on the interfacing only, to ¼" (6mm). From here on out, you'll treat the fabric-and-interfacing combo as a single piece.

4. STITCH COLLAR PIECES TOGETHER

Stitch the two collar pieces with the right sides together using a ⅝" (1.6cm) seam allowance. Sew only along three sides, leaving the curved edge (the neckline) unstitched.

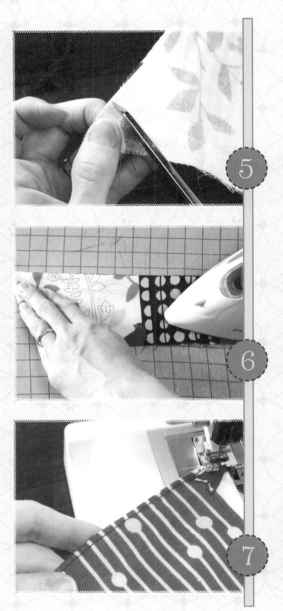

5. TRIM POINTS

Trim out the interfacing on the points to reduce the bulk and clip the points off the collar.

6. TURN RIGHT SIDE OUT AND PRESS

Turn the collar right side out and use the tip of the knitting needle to make the points sharp. As you turn the collar right side out, take a look at the seam line: You want to "cheat" that seam over to one side so it won't show from the top of the collar after the collar has been attached to the blouse. Do this by ever so slightly rolling the seam over to one side so the stitch line lies to the underside by just a hair. The fabric with the interfacing will be the upper, visible-to-the-outside piece of your collar, so cheat the seam to the piece without interfacing so it will lie to the underside of the collar and be hidden from view. Press the collar like crazy so it's nice and crisp.

7. TOPSTITCH COLLAR

Topstitch along the three finished sides of the collar. Stitch ¼" (6mm) from the edge. You can choose to use a contrasting thread that stands out (for a more decorative look) or one that blends in.

Stitch Tip

When topstitching the collar of a blouse, think about the overall look of your project. You might want to repeat the look on the hem and sleeves, too. If you choose to do a contrasting topstitching, set your stitch length slightly longer than usual—this will give the stitches more presence. You can also buy a special topstitching thread, which is slightly thicker and produces the same effect.

The collar stand serves to connect the collar to the neck opening. It's what makes the collar stand up just a bit. Take a look at one of your blouses or a men's dress shirt, and you'll see what I mean. It also adds a little more of a formal, menswear feel to this top, and gives you some flexibility in how you wear it. One collar band, many birds. Or something like that.

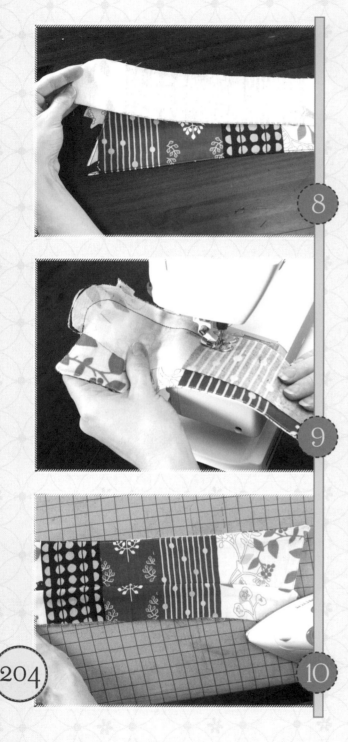

8. LAYER COLLAR AND COLLAR BANDS

Add interfacing (using the method you prefer) to one of the collar stand pieces. Then place the collar stand piece without interfacing right side up. The collar should be right side up. Remember, the right side—or upper side—of your collar is the one on which you can't see the seam line. Place the collar stand with interfacing right sides together with the other collar stand, sandwiching the collar in the middle.

9. STITCH COLLAR AND STAND TOGETHER

Stitch the collar stand pieces together, using a ⅝" (1.6cm) seam allowance, catching the collar in between (along its edge). Stitch around the curved edges and along the collar edge that was open (where you turned it), leaving the bottom edge of the coillar stand unstitched. You'll see that the seam comes right around to connect the collar stand to the collar just at the side—this makes a really clean look in the finished product.

10. TURN RIGHT SIDE OUT AND PRESS

Clip the curves on the collar stand. Turn the collar stand right side out and press, press, press. Isn't that satisfying? OK, time to set the collar aside and move on to the next step.

Tackling the Darts

Darts serve to shape the two-dimensional fabric and make it fit and flatter our three-dimensional bodies. They are one of the most common methods for manipulating fabric in apparel and are really an essential skill if you want to play at the varsity level. Let's tackle a few and you'll see how simple they really are!

1. MARK DOTS ON FABRIC

To start, you'll need the front and back fabric pieces and the matching pattern pieces. Using chalk, mark all bust and waist darts for your size on the wrong side of the fabric. Place a finger on the dot on the pattern, pull back the pattern and then make a mark on the fabric. (You can also work with a sharpened chalk or marking pencil and mark right through the pattern paper if it is thin enough.)

2. CONNECT DOTS

Connect the dots with a ruler. (FYI, for this project our darts are straight, but most commerical patterns have darts that are slightly curved, and you really do get the best results if you can follow that curve. If you can't, though, the darts will still have the right shape—just keep in mind when you stitch that although dots connected with a straight ruler might look like jagged lines, the stitches should make a smooth line.)

3. FOLD FABRIC

Before stitching the darts, you'll need to fold the fabric with the right sides together, matching the dots, and pin in place. Each dart has three sets of lines. The straight line in the center of the dart is the fold line. The angled lines on each side should match when you fold the dart, matching dots, and become the stitching line. Check to be sure that the lines are on top of one another on either side of the fabric by putting a pin through the dot—it should come out the dot on the other side. Keep adjusting your fold until the pin goes through both dots and the lines are where they ought to be.

4. STITCH DARTS

Start stitching the bust darts using the remaining chalk line as a guide. Stitch from the widest part of the dart toward the tip, but don't backtack. You want to get closer and closer to the point and then stitch off the edge. With too sharp a finish you get a pointy bust line, and you want to avoid that.

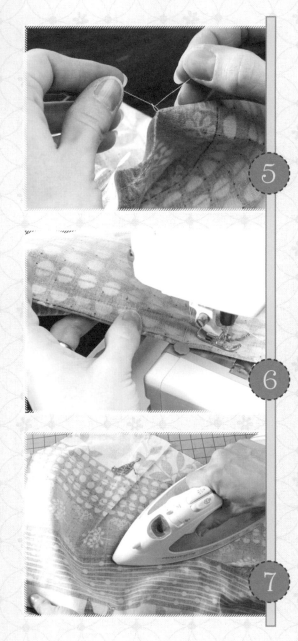

5. DOUBLE KNOT THREAD

When you finish stitching, remove the work from the machine and tie a double knot in the threads to secure the stitches.

6. STITCH WAIST DARTS

Stitch the waist darts (on both the front and the back) in much the same way as the bust darts. Start in the middle at the widest section and then stitch toward the point. Repeat going in the other direction.

7. PRESS DARTS

Press the darts down toward the waistline. As you press the darts, keep in mind that you don't want to create a flattened portion at either end. Instead, you're trying to make a cup for the bust and a curve for the waist. So as you press to the point on each dart, press into the point and move the tip of the iron in such a way that it smooths out the stitching and creates a nice, smooth curve.

Adding the Breast Patch Pocket

Let's mix a little business with our pleasure, shall we? In sewing, as in life, it's the little details that make people really sit up and take notice. For your blouse, you'll add a little pocket to give your top that certain extra something. This pocket is similar to the ones you added to your A-line skirt, but you'll construct it a little differently, just for variety's sake.

1. FOLD TOP EDGE OF POCKET

Place your pocket piece right side down and fold the upper edge to the wrong side ¼" (6mm). Press the fold in place. Now turn the pocket over, so you're looking at the right side, and fold the upper edge—including the ¼" (6mm) you just pressed in place—over by 1" (3cm), with right sides together. Press this second fold in place. Stitch both folds in place only along the sides of the pocket, from top to bottom, but not along the long edge. The goal here is to make an upper edge to the finished pocket that will flip to the wrong side and line everything else up. (Hang in there because in the next step it's all really going to make sense.)

2. TURN RIGHT SIDE OUT

Turn the folded edge right side out. Notice how it tucks the edges under with it to just the right depth. (I love that trick.)

3. FOLD OTHER EDGES

Fold up the remaining three sides, mitering the corners. Press the folds in place. This allows you to line up the sides of the pocket at just the right distance for nice, straight, even stitching.

4. STITCH POCKET TO BLOUSE

Place the pocket on the blouse left front. Be sure to place the folded edge (from step 1) at the top. Stitch the pocket in place along the sides and bottom, leaving the top edge open. Stitch close to the edge of the pocket. (By the way, if you really love pockets, you can always add another on the right, but if you're only doing one, left is totally the way to go.)

Insetting the Sleeves

The sleeves for this pattern are sweet cap sleeves, and have a narrow hem at the lower edge. If you want your sleeves to have a little more body, consider lining the sleeves by cutting out four sleeves and stitching two together for each sleeve prior to attaching them to the blouse.

1. SEW FRONTS TO BACK

Before beginning the sleeves, stitch the two fronts to the blouse back. First, stitch the fronts to the back at the shoulder seams, matching notches and using a ⅝" (1.6cm) seam allowance. Then stitch the side seams, matching notches and following the curve of the waistline. Press your seam allowances open. Your blouse body looks sort of like a vest now.

2. STITCH UNDERARM SEAM

Fold a sleeve in half with the right sides together. Stitch the short underarm seam using a ⅝" (1.6cm) seam allowance.

3. STITCH HEM

Fold up the hem on the lower edge of the sleeve: If you've edge finished the lower edge of the sleeve, fold the whole thing under ⅝" (1.6cm). If you haven't, fold under ¼" (6mm) then another ½" (1.3cm), pressing after each fold. This will trap the unfinished edges inside and give you a clean hem at the sleeve. Press the hem. Stitch the hem in place close to the edge of the sleeve. Use the same thread as you used in the topstitching on the collar (see page 203), if you like.

4. EASE STITCH TOP OF SLEEVE

Because your shoulder is curved you have to create more volume at the top of the sleeve for your shoulder to fit into, or else you'll always be squeezed by the sleeve. You do this by ease stitching: running gathering stitches at the top of the sleeve that allow you to create teeny tiny gathers that will make a slightly rounded shape at the top of your shoulder. You don't want to make a puffed sleeve—these gathers will vanish when you stitch the sleeve in place. (Really.)

Ease stitch the upper edge of the sleeve cap between notches using your longest straight stitch and a ⅝" (1.6cm) seam allowance. It's really important that the first row of ease stitches is at the seam line because this will help them disappear the best. Run two more rows of ease stitches, both inside the seam allowance. (For more on ease stitching, see page 198.)

5. ADJUST EASE

Pull the ease stitching threads to adjust the ease on your sleeve cap to reduce the fullness.

6. PLACE SLEEVE IN SLEEVE OPENING

Place the sleeve in the sleeve opening on the blouse, matching notches and underarm seams, and the dot on top of the sleeve to the shoulder seam. (Remembert, you have one left and one right sleeve. Use the notches you cut to help you put the correct one on each side of the blouse: single notch for shirt front, double notch for shirt back.) Adjust the ease as needed to fit by adding and removing gathers at the sleeve cap.

7. STITCH SLEEVE IN PLACE

After the sleeve and sleeve opening are the same size, pin them in place. Stitch the two together using a ⁵⁄₈" (1.6cm) seam allowance. As you stitch, move the fullness of the ease stitching to the seam allowance side and watch as the gathers disappear! This can be a tricky step and requires some patience on your part, but a well-set sleeve always looks couture.

8. TURN RIGHT SIDE OUT AND PRESS

Turn the sleeve right side out. Press the seam allowances toward the sleeve because that's the direction you'll be putting your arm in the hole.

Repeat steps 2–8 to complete the other sleeve.

Attaching the Front Facing and Collar

We've talked here and there already about facings. Their purpose in many patterns is to finish off an edge, as well as give support to a garment. That's what you're using them for in this project. Because you're adding buttons at the front of the blouse, you want to be sure that there is enough fabric behind each button and buttonhole to properly support them while giving the blouse its shape—you'll use a facing plus some interfacing to achieve that.

1. ATTACH FRONT FACING TO BLOUSE FRONT

Apply interfacing (either sew-in or fusible) to the wrong sides of both of the front facings. Then place the right front facing right sides together with the right side of the blouse front. Stitch the facing to the blouse along the long edge using a $5/8$" (1.6cm) seam allowance. Repeat to attach the left front facing.

2. UNDERSTITCH FACING

Understitch the seam allowances of the facings. (For more on understitching, see page 196.) Turn both facings to the inside. Press, press, press!

3. STAYSTITCH COLLAR OPENING

Staystitching is a technique that uses a row of stitches through a single layer of fabric to hold the shape of the garment so it doesn't get distorted when attaching it to another pattern piece. In this case, as you attach the collar stand to the collar opening, you don't want to stretch the curved opening to the point that the collar won't fit properly anymore. Using your default stitch length, run a single row of straight stitches at a $3/8$" (1cm) seam allowance all the way around the collar opening.

4. PIN COLLAR TO FACING

The facing pieces that you just stitched have two basic functions: They create a finished edge for the front of the blouse, and they trap the collar at the upper, curved edge. To attach the collar, turn the collar facing (the curved part of the front facing) back to the outside. Pin the collar stand to the upper neck edge starting at the centers (which should match up) and continuing out to the seam where the facings are stitched to the shirt fronts. The collar band should fit neatly right up against the seam at the shirt front on both the right and left. If it doesn't, adjust each side—again, from the center and evenly—until they do.

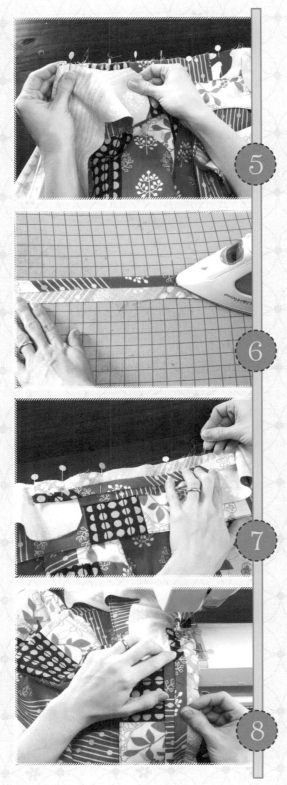

5. FOLD FACING AND PIN

Fold the front facing to cover the front edges of the collar band. Pin in place.

6. CUT AND FOLD BIAS TAPE

Do you see how at the back of the collar stand there's a big, fat opening that has unfinished edges? You need to finish those to make the garment complete. Many patterns take you down a complicated route of snipping into the collar and folding it back, and then tucking your seam allowances underneath it, but I think that's way too time-consuming and doesn't really look that good. Instead, we're going to cover the raw edges with bias tape. Because you know how to make bias tape! If you want to super-sass it up, consider using a contrasting fabric here—a little surprise that will peek out every now and then!

Begin by cutting a piece of bias tape that measures 1¼" (3cm) wide by 5' (13cm) long. You don't need to make CBT for this step—just find the bias line on the fabric you'd like to use at the back of the neck (it can totally be a scrap), and snip off the length you need. Fold one long edge of the bias tape ¼" (6mm) and press in place. Leave the other edge unpressed.

7. PLACE BIAS TAPE OVER FACING AND COLLAR

Place the raw edge of the bias tape along the neckline, over the facing ends and over the collar. You should have a stack of fabrics at this point.

8. STITCH ON COLLAR

Stitch the collar on through all the layers—bias tape, collar and facing—using a ⅝" (1.6cm) seam allowance. Be careful to keep all the layers nice and flat while you stitch.

211

9. TRIM SEAM ALLOWANCE

Flip the collar to the inside. You'll see how the facings lie down and the bias tape covers the seam allowance. If any seam allowance is peeking out, trim it to ¼" (6mm).

10. PRESS BIAS TAPE

Press the bias tape in place over the seam allowances at the back of the neck, between the two facings.

11. STITCH

Start stitching very close to the folded edge of the bias tape. As you continue stitching be careful of the shape of the neckline. When you stitched the bias tape on initially, it was easy to treat the seam as a straight line. But now you're really following the curve of the neckline. Stretch the collar in an arc, along the natural curve of the neckline. As you stitch the bias tape down, catch the facings in your stitches, and place your stitch line very close to the folded edge of the bias tape. Be prepared to stop and start a bit, and as you do, keep sweeping your hand under the rest of the blouse to make sure it stays smooth under the needle. This will give you the best, cleanest finish on the back of the blouse when your collar is in!

Stitch Tip

If you aren't careful to keep moving the body of the blouse out of the way underneath the work as you stitch, you're likely to make folds and tucks (shown here) where there shouldn't be any.

Stitching the Buttons and Buttonholes

I like to use covered buttons for some projects, especially the ones where the fabric is so wonderful I just want to see more of it. Covered buttons come in kits with a mold, a pusher and button forms and are a snap to make (if you'll pardon the pun). You can use covered or regular buttons for your blouse.

1. OPTIONAL: MAKE COVERED BUTTONS

If desired, make covered buttons using a package of buttons to cover and the blouse fabric. Follow the instructions on the package to make the buttons.

2. MARK PLACEMENT OF BUTTONS AND BUTTONHOLES

If you haven't already, mark the placement of the six buttons and buttonholes using the pattern symbols as a guide. Then stitch the buttonholes using your machine's buttonhole foot and setting. (For a reminder on how to stitch buttonholes, see pages 133–135.)

3. SEW ON BUTTONS

If you've made covered buttons, hand sew the buttons on. Be sure to tie a knot in the thread behind the buttons to ensure they don't fall off! If you're using regular sew-on buttons, you can hand or machine stitch them to the blouse.

Button Conventions

There are conventions about where buttons and buttonholes ought to go. Most patterns use these hidden rules when putting marks on the pattern to indicate where a button or buttonhole ought to be, but be aware that the size of the button makes a difference. So if you use a different button size from what the pattern calls for, you'll need to adjust the markings.
Buttonholes are slightly larger than the buttons and are placed half the width of the button from the edge of the garment. And the buttons themselves shouldn't be centered in the buttonhole, but ought to be set so that when the garment is worn, the button slides naturally to the far end, preventing gaping. Finally, for women's shirts, buttonholes go on the left, and for men's shirts, they go on the right.

Hemming the Curved Edge

A curved hem requires a little different handling than a straight hem. Like the top of your sleeve cap, there is more fullness at the bottom of the curves than on the edge to which you'll stitch it. You need to take that fullness out in order to get the hem to lie smoothly. You'll do that the same way you did the sleeves on this blouse and the hem on your A-line skirt: with ease stitching.

1. STITCH HEM AND STITCH EDGE OF FACING

Finish off the lower edge of the blouse with a zigzag stitch along the raw edge. Then run one line of ease stitches along the edge at ⅜" (1cm). Leave long ends on the threads.

Fold the lower edge of your facing right sides together with the shirt front below the last buttonhole. Stitch a straight seam parallel to the hemline at ⅝" (1.6cm). Clip the corner. Fold the facing back to the inside and press. This seems like a crazy step, but it makes for a prettier, more professional hem when viewed from the front of your blouse. This step is really similar to what we did at the top edge of your pocket: You're creating a little "pouch" that will flip back to the inside (i.e., wrong sides together) and establish the hemline, but that from the outside of the garment will look clean and finished.

2. EASE OUT FULLNESS IN HEM

Turn up the remaining length of the hem ⅝" (1.6cm). Use your ease stitching to ease out the excess fullness in the curves until the hem will lie flat. Press the fold in place

3. STITCH HEM IN PLACE

Stitch the hem close to the zigzag edge on top of the zigzag stitching. Begin at the very edge of the blouse front, and continue all the way over to the other blouse front.

No matter how many times I make something to wear, I always feel an immense sense of satisfaction when I sit back and look at what I've done. Regardless of how simple or fancy you've made your blouse, I think you deserve a moment to rest on your laurels, admire what you've done, and congratulate yourself. You, my friend, now officially have Mad Skillz.

FOR MORE INSPIRATION

As with pretty much all the other projects, there are many variations to make! Suddenly, ruffles are everywhere, and they look fantastic on the front of this blouse (on the left). Just cut strips of your blouse fabric, press under the long edges and stitch to finish, and then run a gathering stitch down the center to create a ruffle. Stitch them to the front of the blouse before adding the collar, beginning at the front facing and working your way out. On the variation on the right, I've widened both the blouse fronts and then pulled in the shape with pintucks for a little old-school shaping.

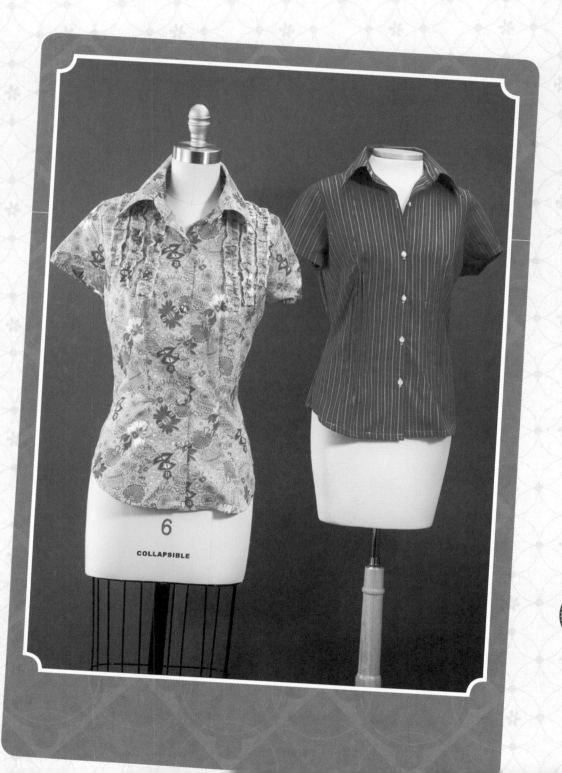

CONCLUSION

You've done so much in these pages. And truly: You've really just seen the tip of the iceberg. Sewing is such an amazing gift—one where if you have the skills, you can truly create anything you can dream up. I've worked hard to offer you a list of skills that will give you a well-stocked toolbox to go out and dream big. Have fun!

I spend giant portions of my days thinking about sewing; you don't have to feel that way in order for this to be something you love. My goal in these pages has been to give you the skills and tools you need to explore where sewing can fit into your life and your days—and I hope you've found plenty of places where this is something you want to pursue and embrace. You're part of something much bigger than you and are connected to people from the deep past, from your own past and on into your present and future. Welcome, and happy stitching!

RESOURCES AND INSPIRATION

Blogs and Web sites

FOR IDEAS AND INSPIRATION:

Amanda's Adventures in Sewing
amandasadventuresinsewing.blogspot.com

Burda Style (for downloadable patterns)
www.burdastyle.com/patterns

Casey's Elegant Musings
blog.caseybrowndesigns.com

Elsie Marley
www.elsiemarley.com

Fehr Trade
www.fehrtrade.com

Gertie's New Blog for Better Sewing
www.blogforbettersewing.com

MADE
www.dana-made-it.com

Made by Rae
madebyrae.blogspot.com

The Selfish Seamstress
selfishseamstress.wordpress.com

Katie Did
katiedid.squarespace.com

The Long Thread
thelongthread.com

SouleMama
www.soulemama.com/soulemama

Wardrobe Refashion
nikkishell.typepad.com/wardroberefashion

FABRIC AND PATTERN DESIGNERS' BLOGS:

Heather Bailey
heatherbailey.typepad.com

Disdressed
disdressed.blogspot.com

Genevieve Gail
genevievegail.blogspot.com

Anna Maria Horner
annamariahorner.blogspot.com

Lizzy House
lizzyhouse.typepad.com

Heather Ross
heatherross.squarespace.com

Patty Young
modkidboutique.blogspot.com

Reference books worth the investment:

Reader's Digest Guide to Sewing, any edition pre-1978 (Reader's Digest Association)
Sew Everything Workshop by Diana Rupp (Workman Publishing, 2007)
Sew U by Wendy Mullin (Bulfinch Press, 2006)
The Sewing Book by Allison Smith (DK Publishing, 2009)
The Sewing Bible by Ruth Singer (Potter Craft, 2008)

❉ GLOSSARY

appliqué: a decorative sewing technique that applies (hence the name) small pieces of fabric on top of a base fabric to create designs and shapes

backtacking (or backstitching): reverse stitching over an area previously stitched to create a "knot" that will hold your seam in place

baste: temporary stitches used in place of pins to hold fabric together while constructing or fitting a project

bias line: the 45-degree line across the grain and crossgrain of fabric where the fibers exhibit the most give and stretch

bias tape: a strip of fabric cut on the bias, with edges pressed under to create binding or edging for projects

bias tape maker: a device used with an iron to press in the edges of bias tape to a regular seam allowance

blind hem: hemming technique that allows you to place a hem with nearly no thread showing on the public side of the garment; can be completed using a specialty presser foot

bobbin: small spool that fits below the throat plate of the sewing machine to hold the lower thread for the lockstitch mechanism

buttonhole stitch: a special stitch on many sewing machines that will create a buttonhole of a predetermined size

casing: a channel through which elastic, drawstrings and trims can pass; used most at waistbands and openings of bags

chain stitching: a technique that allows you to stitch a seam, place another fabric below the presser foot and stitch another seam connected to the first by a short "chain" of free stitches; often used to speed up quilting and other sewing tasks that utilize many short seams

channel stitch: stitching designed to divide one section of a project from another, as in making a pocket

charm pack: a precut bundle of fabric measuring 5" × 5" (13cm × 13cm) and containing forty-two squares; each fabric square is different from the others

clipping corners and curves: snipping into the seam allowance of a seam in order to reduce bulk when the project is turned right side out; snip up to but not through the stitches

continuous bias tape: a technique for creating greater yardage of bias tape by stitching a tube and cutting it into a spiral of one unbroken strip

crossgrain: the weft of the fabric; at a 90-degree angle to the selvage/grainline

dart: used to reduce bulk in a garment by shaping the two-dimensional fabric to fit the three-dimensional body beneath it; usually seen at bust and waist

double thickness: two layers of fabric stacked on top of one another; usually right sides together

ease stitching: stitches used to adjust fullness at hemlines; run a basting stitch, then draw up the fullness to match your other edge

edge finish: any technique that "seals" the threads along one edge of a piece of fabric; may be completed with a zigzag stitch, serger or folding

elastic: knit or woven with stretch, used to draw in fabric and hold it to a particular size, usually at waistbands, sleeves and in decorative applications

expandable measure: used to mark placement of elements at regular intervals, like buttonholes and pleats

facing: piece of fabric used to finish an edge of a garment; usually cut to mirror the shape of the outer, public garment edge and stitched right sides together; often used at shirt front, collar edges and waistbands

fat quarter: cut of fabric measuring 18" × 22" (46cm × 56cm) and equivalent to half of a half yard; very popular quilting and crafting cut

feed dogs: sewing machine part beneath the throat plate that interacts with the presser foot to move fabric through the machine from front to back

free-motion quilting: sewing technique that allows you to "drive" the thread over the fabric and control more directly how much thread is deposited in particular places on the project

fusible webbing: commercial product that creates a fabric "sticker" by placing two-sided heat-activated glue on one piece of fabric to allow it to adhere to another fabric; used for decorative sewing and machine appliqué

gather: fabric-shaping technique that creates small puffs in fabric and reduces the overall length by drawing it up; gathers should be full, and when stitched, should resemble flattened U's

grainline: the threads in a fabric that are parallel to the selvage edge; the fabric warp

gutter stitch: stitches placed exactly on top of the stitches of a previous seam; intended to create an invisible line of stitches; also called "stitch the ditch"

hem: lower edge of a garment after it is finished; most hems involve folding the fabric to the wrong side and securing with stitches

hem guide: ruled device used to measure the consistent depth of a hem on a garment; can also be used for other, non-clothing projects

interfacing: man-made product, with or without heat-activated glue, that provides body and shape to projects; comes in a wide variety of weights to suit nearly any sewing project

invisible zipper: closure that uses plastic teeth on polyester tape to turn seam edges to the inside and create an unnoticeable entry point for a garment

lining: fabric cut to the shape of a project and used to completely cover the inside in an identical form

machine bed: the lower level of a sewing machine, where the throat plate sits and where most of the work gets done

machine head: the upper portion of a sewing machine, where the needle bar is located, and which is directly attached to the motor

matching side seams: ensuring that seams stitched at either side of a project meet one another exactly to create a clean finish

mitered corner: corner where fabrics meet at a 45-degree angle for a clean, professional finish

needle bar: the part of your sewing machine that carries the needle up and down by way of the motor

on-seam pocket: pocket that is placed on the side of a garment and is invisible to view

overcast edge: finish that uses zigzag stitches to prevent fabric from unraveling

patch pocket: pocket that is attached to the surface of a project or garment, rather than along a seam

piping: trim that goes within a seam and is stuffed with cording to create a rounded look

pivot: turning sharply at a corner to continue a row of stitches around a corner

pleat: method of manipulating fabric by folding and laying the fold down flat to one side

presser foot: sewing machine part that holds the fabric against the feed dogs to allow it to move through the machine

presser foot lever: lowers and raises the presser foot; usually located at the back of the machine head

right side: the "public" side of a piece of fabric

right sides together: placing the two public sides of two fabrics touching one another

seam: line along which two fabrics are stitched to one another

seam allowance: the excess fabric at the outside of a seam that provides a margin to keep stitches in place

selvage (or selvedge): the finished edge of fabric where it has come off the loom

slip stitch: hand stitch designed to create an invisible finish at a seam line

stabilizer: man-made heat-activated product that prevents shifting of fabric while stiching; used primarily for machine embroiery and applique

stitch the ditch: see gutter stitch

take-up lever: machine part that controls the thread on its way toward the needle bar

tension: the firmess in thread as it moves from the spool to the needle

thread guides: small metal loops or fingers on the sewing machine that direct the thread and prevent tangling during sewing

true up: squaring up the fabric grain for more perfect results

throat plate: the metal plate on the machine bed that indicates distance from the needle and allows the needle to pass through to the bobbin below

topstitch: visible stitching, usually parallel to a seam, that is intended to be seen

understitching: stitches designed to anchor facings in place; they are hidden in the facing and seam allowance of a project

universal zipper: standard closure with plastic teeth and polyester tapes

wrong side: the non-public side of a piece of fabric

wrong sides together: placing the two non-public sides of fabric touching one another

yoke: fitted section of a garment that attaches to the rest of the garment; often used on shirts and skirts

zigzag stitch: stitches that move from left to right and are used in deocrative applications, for buttonholes and in machine appliqué

�֍ INDEX

❋ ABOUT THE AUTHOR

Deborah Moebes began sewing at the age of seven when her mother first showed her how to thread a needle. In college, she worked in the university costume shop and was exposed to a whole new level of sewing and detail, which revolutionized her view of what she might be able to stitch. After nearly ten years of teaching in the public school system, a graduate degree in archaeology, and a little globe-trotting, Deborah began designing children's clothing, which led to teaching sewing classes through a local designer's co-op. Those small classes have grown into Whipstitch Lounge, a popular in-town Atlanta sewing destination, and Whipstitch Fabrics, a successful online fabric shop. Deborah lives in the city of Atlanta with her husband and their 3.5 children.

You can visit Deborah at www.whipstitchfabrics.com.

ABOUT THE CD

You'll find the following pattern files on the CD:

- Relaxing Eye Mask
- Hipster Belt
- A-Line Skirt, Size 4
- A-Line Skirt, Size 6
- A-Line Skirt, Size 8
- A-Line Skirt, Size 10
- A-Line Skirt, Size 12
- A-Line Skirt, Size 14
- Carport Skirt, Size 4
- Carport Skirt, Size 6
- Carport Skirt, Size 8
- Carport Skirt, Size 10
- Carport Skirt, Size 12
- Carport Skirt, Size 14
- Cap-Sleeved Blouse, all sizes

The format of the patterns included on the CD is slightly different than what you might be expecting, and there are some reasons for that.

First, I've met so many new stitchers who feel intimidated by a tissue paper pattern, the kind that comes in the envelope from the fabric shop. Their fear is that they'll cut it out wrong and ruin the pattern forever, and it gives them a kind of deer-in-headlights feeling as they approach a project. Since I would vastly prefer that you jump in and discover you can do a lot more than you think you can, I really wanted these patterns to have a different format, one that would eliminate that concern by allowing you to print them over and over, and make mistakes without worry.

Second, there are so many new pattern resources out there (and a bunch of them are listed in the Resources section of the book) that use downloadable patterns, most of them free of charge. Yippee! But what if you've only ever used tissue patterns and the free ones look so strange to you that you're prevented from really taking advantage of all the great stuff that's out there, the really modern, edgy stuff that appeals to you most?

So the patterns are all presented in a PDF format and tiled. What that means is that each pattern piece is larger than a single sheet of 8½" × 11" (22cm × 28cm) printer paper, but to help you print them on a regular printer, they are split on multiple sheets. Your job is to print them out and then put them together. The benefit is that you can repeat this procedure over and over, and avoid needing to store a pattern (unless you choose) while also knowing that if you do make a mistake, it's a snap to fix!

Insert the CD into your computer to retrieve the instructions for printing and using the patterns. (Note that if you want, you can send these files electronically to a print shop and have them printed on a single, large-format page.)

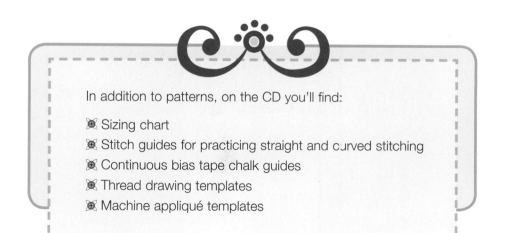

In addition to patterns, on the CD you'll find:

- Sizing chart
- Stitch guides for practicing straight and curved stitching
- Continuous bias tape chalk guides
- Thread drawing templates
- Machine appliqué templates

STITCH MORE GREAT PROJECTS WITH THESE OTHER KRAUSE PUBLICATIONS

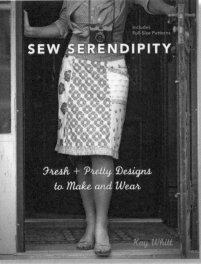

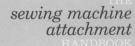

JOEL DEWBERRY'S SEWN SPACES
JOEL DEWBERRY

Whether you're a crafter, sewer, quilter or style seeker you'll love the distinctive looks with simple how-to fabric projects and loads of inspiration. If you're interested in delivering a fresh approach to styling your life that is accessible and easily accomplished, then *Sewn Spaces* is for you.

paperback; 9" × 9.5"; 128 pages
ISBN-10: 0-89689-924-1
   ISBN-13: 978-0-89689-924-7
   SRN: Z3608

SEW SERENDIPITY
KAY WHITT

With *Sew Serendipity*, you'll find out how to lay out the pattern pieces, cut them out and sew them up. All you have to do is put them on and strut your stuff! The book provides the master instructions for each basic garment, and individual instruction for each unique look. Once you master the basics, changing it up is a snap! Included in the book are tissue pattern inserts, and each clothing pattern is graded in seven sizes.

paperback; 8" × 10"; 160 pages
ISBN-10: 1-4402-0357-1
ISBN-13: 978-1-4402-0357-2
SRN: Z4958

THE SEWING MACHINE ATTACHMENT HANDBOOK
BY CHARLENE PHILLIPS

Sewing machine attachments don't have to be scary. With *The Sewing Machine Attachment Handbook*, you'll gain the knowledge you need to conquer that box of metal and plastic. This indispensable guide will help you identify 25+ of the most common attachment feet and accessories with detailed illustrations and pictures, including rufflers, binders, hemmers and more.

paperback; 8" × 8"; 144 pages
ISBN-10: 0-8968-9923-3
ISBN-13: 978-0-8968-9923-0
SRN: Z3607

These and other fine Krause Publications titles are available at your local craft retailer, bookstore or online supplier, or visit our Web site at **www.mycraftivitystore.com**.